C000008374

THE BRISTOL AVON
A Pictorial History

From Source to Avonmouth

Raymond Thompson took this photograph of his wife, Gwendoline, daughter, Valmai, and sister-in-law, Marion Payne, aboard an old boat moored at Saltford in 1944.

THE BRISTOL AVON
A Pictorial History

From Source to Avonmouth

Josephine Jeremiah

Phillimore

2005

Published by
PHILLIMORE & CO. LTD,
Shopwyke Manor Barn, Chichester, West Sussex, England

© Josephine Jeremiah, 2005

ISBN 1 86077 362 1

Printed and bound in Great Britain by
CAMBRIDGE PRINTING

List of Illustrations

Frontispiece: Old boat, Saltford, 1944

ACKNOWLEDGEMENTS

My thanks go to the following for their help in enabling me to compile this book:
Archive CD Books, Edna Marlow in Ottawa, Clare Williams in Sydney and Ian Jeremiah.

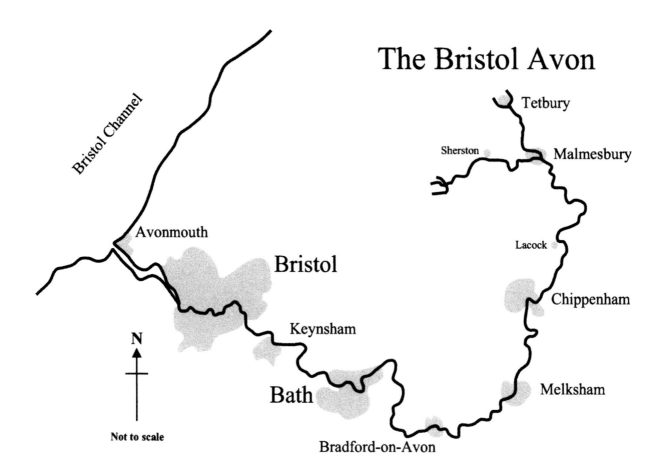

The Bristol Avon

Tetbury

Sherston

Malmesbury

Avonmouth

Bristol Channel

Bristol

Lacock

Chippenham

Keynsham

N

Bath

Melksham

Not to scale

Bradford-on-Avon

An Historical Journey

The Bristol Avon is my home river. As a child, I travelled down it, by paddle steamer, from Hotwells to Clevedon. I crossed it, via the Clifton Suspension Bridge, to see the bluebells in Leigh Woods and travelled over Bedminster Bridge, on countless day trips, to Weston-super-Mare. As a teenager, I spent lazy days on the river bank at Hanham and enjoyed winter picnics in Hanham Woods. Later, in my adult years, I boated on the river. More recently, I have delved into the history of the river not only in the locations near my family home, but in the towns and villages further upstream and those near its source. My study of the River Avon and its surroundings has been concentrated mainly on the period between the late 18th century and the early 20th century as that is where my family history interests lie. During this time, my ancestors lived along the river and their occupations included waterman, steam packet captain, steam packet porter, shipwright, sail maker, dockman, lockman and Pill pilot.

The actual source of the Bristol Avon, which rises in Gloucestershire, is debatable. Above Malmesbury, there are two branches of the river, one named on Ordnance Survey maps as River Avon (Tetbury Branch) and the other as River Avon (Sherston Branch). Referring to these branches of the river at Malmesbury, the 16th-century writer, John Leland, noted:

> Newton water cummith a 2 miles from north to the toun; and Avon water cummith by weste of the toun from Lokington a 4 miles of, and meete about a bridge at south est part of the toun and so goith Avon by south a while, and then turneth flat west toward Bristow.

Newton is a variation in spelling for Newnton, the northern branch of the river passing near Long Newnton south-east of Tetbury. In his *New History of Gloucestershire* (1779), Samuel Rudder stated that the rivulet separating the counties of Gloucestershire and Wiltshire at Tetbury was 'unquestionably the head, or highest source of the Bristol Avon'. The Rev. Alfred T. Lee, in *The History of the Town and Parish of Tetbury* (1857), was also of the opinion that Tetbury was the source of the river, maintaining, 'The Bristol Avon takes its rise from the spring in Magdalen Meadow'. According to Ordnance Survey maps, the source of the Tetbury Avon is Wor Well to the north-east of Tetbury.

The Sherston Avon is said, by some, to rise in the grounds of Badminton Park and flow past Luckington, Leland's 'Lokington', though the distance between that village and Malmesbury is rather more than Leland's estimate of four miles. Ernest Walls, in *The Bristol Avon* (1927), decided that a spring, half a mile or less from the bridge below Luckington's church, was the 'authentic source of the Sherston Avon'. Ordnance Survey maps, however, name a different stream, to the north-west of Sherston, as the River Avon (Sherston Branch).

Whichever stream leads from the real source, the two branches of the River Avon encircle the hill-top town of Malmesbury and meet a short distance below St John's Bridge to the south-east of the town. From Malmesbury, the River Avon, sometimes called the Lower Avon, flows in a southerly direction to the market town of Chippenham. Continuing on the same course, it passes the National Trust village of Lacock and the town of Melksham before first turning to the south-west and then to the north-west through the town of Bradford-on-Avon and the cities of Bath and Bristol. Finally, it makes its way through the spectacular Avon Gorge to the Severn estuary at Avonmouth.

At Tetbury, the infant River Avon flows under the Wiltshire Bridge, which was formerly the boundary between Gloucestershire and Wiltshire. Samuel Rudder noted that, in winter, its waters were augmented by another little stream, but that in the summer months these rivulets were dry. In the past, Tetbury suffered from a lack of water because of its high location. Its inhabitants used to purchase water at 6d. and even 10d. a hogshead until, in 1749, an ancient well, in the wool market, was deepened. Samuel Rudder remarked that woollen cloth was formerly made in Tetbury, but manufacture declined because of the need for constant water to drive the fulling mills. In 1779, the author commented: 'The chief manufactures now carried on here, are woolstapling and woolcombing, in which latter about one hundred and fifty persons find constant employment; and the combed wool is sold at Coventry, Kidderminster, Leicester and other markets.' In 1783, there were 18 wool staplers in Tetbury.

In 1857, the Rev. Alfred T. Lee described the location of this Cotswold market town in *The History of the Town and Parish of Tetbury*:

> The town of Tetbury stands on an elevated and commanding situation, on the high road between Bath and Oxford. On the whole it is well built, and many of the houses are of considerable antiquity. It consists principally of a Long Street, crossed at right angles by two shorter ones, that on the North side leading to the spacious area, called the Chipping (in which the market was formerly held, and in which the remains of the old Cistercian Monastery may be seen); that on the South to the Parish Church from whence it derives its name.

At the meeting of Tetbury's main streets, a notable attraction of the town is the Market House, underneath which markets are still held. Originally erected in 1655, this large market house was formerly used for a Wednesday market where the chief article for sale was yarn. Cheese, bacon and other commodities were once sold in great quantities in a smaller market house. Another striking feature of the town is the tall pinnacled tower and elegant spire of the parish church. Tetbury's parish church, apart from its tower and spire, had been demolished in 1777 and a new church was constructed, which was opened in 1781. The tower and spire were both rebuilt in the 1890s and restoration of the church has taken place in more recent times during 1992-3.

The square central tower of Sherston's parish church of the Holy Cross is a landmark, too. Sherston, also known as Sherston Magna, is along the branch of the River Avon that carries its name. Norman and Early English styles of architecture can be seen in the church and there are some 15th-century windows. A stone figure on the outside of the two-storeyed 15th-century porch is traditionally held to be that of John Rattlebone, but others believe it is the figure of a priest. Legend has it that Rattlebone was a Saxon who fought with Edmund Ironside against Canute, in the Battle of Sherston in 1016, and died of his wounds. Even though some historians believe that this battle occurred in a different place, wherever the location, the *Rattlebone Inn* at Sherston is named after this local hero. The village is said to have once had 15 pubs. Among these were the *Swan*, the *Forester's Arms* and the *Angel*, an old coaching inn. Village industries in the late 19th century included silk manufacture and tanning. Located near the bridge over the Avon, the tannery was closed down in the early 20th century. The slope leading down to the bridge and the river is still known as Tanners Hill.

At Malmesbury, the Tetbury Avon is known locally as the Ingleburn. From Stainsbridge an interesting walk may be taken along its banks, which gives a view of the north aspect of the abbey favoured by late 18th- and early 19th-century artists. Centuries ago, Malmesbury was famous for its mitred Benedictine abbey and this monastic establishment became very rich in medieval times. The abbey was originally founded in the 7th century by Aldhelm who later became Bishop of Sherborne and was canonised. After Aldhelm's burial at Malmesbury, the abbey became a place of pilgrimage.

William of Malmesbury, a 12th-century monk of the abbey, is renowned for his *Gesta regum Anglorum*, a history of the kings of England from A.D. 449 to 1127. In this work, there is an account of an 11th-century monk of Malmesbury Abbey called Eilmer who, wearing wings, launched himself from the top of the tower of a previous abbey church. This attempt to fly ended with Eilmer breaking both his legs and his belief that, if he had used a tail as well, his flight would have been more successful. William of Malmesbury told this story when writing about Eilmer's sighting of a comet in 1066, later known as Halley's Comet, which was thought to be an omen concerning the Norman invasion of England by William the Conqueror.

The present 12th-century abbey survived the Dissolution of the Monasteries though many of the monastic buildings were destroyed. For a time, the nave is said to have been used as a workshop for the cloth trade before William Stumpe, the rich clothier who had acquired it, gave the building to the townspeople for their parish church. In past times, the woollen trade was important to Malmesbury. John Leland noted, in 1542, that 3,000 cloths were made in the town every year. Clothiers worked most of the mills on the edges of Malmesbury during the late 16th and early 17th

1   Burton Hill Mill, near St John's Bridge, was built c.1790 and was once one of the town's woollen mills. It later made silk. Local people still know these former mill buildings as the Silk Mills.

centuries. In *A History of Malmesbury* (1968), Dr Bernulf Hodge observed how some of the old street names referred to this bygone trade, mentioning Blanchard's Green, a place for fulling the cloth, and Katifer Lane, a distortion of 'Chat de Fer' or 'Iron Cat', a large flat iron which was used to smooth the cloth.

The woollen trade came into prominence again at the end of the 18th century when Cannop's Mill was purchased by Francis Hill who had come from Bradford-on-Avon, another Wiltshire town involved in woollen manufacturing. He erected a new woollen mill on the site, which was called Burton Hill Mill. Having increased in size, by 1803, this mill produced superfine broadcloth. In the mid-19th century, the premises were bought by Thomas Bridget & Co. of Derby and became a silk manufactory producing ribbons. The Silk Mills, near St John's Bridge, are now used for residential purposes.

Not far from Malmesbury's Silk Mills, the northern and the western branches of the Avon unite and flow southwards past the villages of Little Somerford, Great Somerford and Christian Malford, the churches of the latter two settlements being close to the river. Before Chippenham is reached, a bridge crosses the Avon at Kellaways. A raised path on arches, at each end of the bridge, enables travellers to pass in safety at times of flood. In the vicinity is a raised causeway, constructed in 1474, extending from Chippenham Cliff to Wick Hill over a distance of about four and a half miles. Maud Heath's Causeway is said to have been provided by a market woman of that name who found the walk to Chippenham across swampy ground inconvenient. She gave property to trustees to ensure that the causeway was kept in good repair for those who came after her. Over the years, the causeway was extended and renewed.

Chippenham was founded in Saxon times. Its name may come from Cyppa's Hamm, the meadow of Cyppa enclosed by the river. The town grew up within a horseshoe bend of the river. Its location by the River Avon was a factor in the development of the cloth industry in the town during medieval times. Chippenham went on to became one of the important centres for wool manufacture in Wiltshire from where much broadcloth was exported during the 14th and 15th centuries. Woollen manufacture was a cottage industry with clothiers distributing the wool first to the spinners, then to the weavers and dyers. *Bailey's Western and Midland Directory* of 1783 lists six clothiers in the town. They were John Reeve Edridge, John Figgins, Thomas Goldney, Matthew Humphreys, Luke Ladd and William Tarrant. Richard Singer & Co. were listed as being 'Manufacturers of Superfine Cloth and Cassameers'. The industry underwent a change when Waterford Cloth Mill and Bridge Cloth Mill came into existence, but, by the late 19th century, the woollen trade had declined in Chippenham as it had in other woollen manufacturing towns in the West Country.

2   Maud Heath's Causeway, Kellaways, 2004. The inscription on the tall stone at the causeway reads:

> To the memory of the worthy MAUD HEATH of Langley Burrell widow who in the year of Grace 1474 for the good of Travellers did in Charity bestow in land and houses about Eight pounds a year forever to be laid out in the Highways and Causeway leading from Wick Hill to Chippenham Clift. This pillar was set up by the feoffees in 1688. Injure me not.

3   This old postcard shows a peaceful view of the river from the mill at Chippenham, *c*.1918. A scene like this was a world away from the horrors of the Great War, which had probably been experienced by the sender who was a serviceman in the Red Cross Hospital in Chippenham.

The Universal British Directory of Trade, Commerce and Manufacture (1791) described Chippenham as 'a pleasant and thriving little borough, situated on the River Avon, over which it has a handsome bridge of sixteen arches'. At this time, Chippenham was a staging post for coaches from London to Bath and Bristol and also from Bath to Oxford. The coaches changed horses at the *White Hart*, *Angel* and *White Lion*, the first two being the principal inns and the latter being the post office. Waggons, between London and Bristol, also came this way. Wiltshire's stopped at the *Bear Inn*, while James's went to the *George Inn* and Porter's to the *Three Crowns*.

A different form of transport came to Chippenham in the form of canal boats on the Wilts & Berks Canal, which was opened in 1810. This canal ran from Semington Junction, on the Kennet & Avon Canal, to Abingdon, on the River Thames, and had a two-mile-long branch to Chippenham. The town initially benefited from Somerset coal being carried along the canal, but the working out of the Somerset coalfield and the coming of the railways added to the decline of the waterway. Arnold Platts, in *A History of Chippenham A.D. 1853-1946*, mentioned a Chippenham canal boatman, John Trow, who used to take his narrowboat, *Helen*, up and down the canal, carrying coal and bricks. John Trow was 75 years old, when he died in 1921, and would have been among the last boatmen to use the canal for transport as the Wilts & Berks Canal was closed in 1914.

Another change in transport was heralded by the construction of the Great Western Railway, which was opened from London to Chippenham in May 1841. The arrival of the railway led to the setting up of railway engineering works by Rowland Brotherhood, a railway engineer working for Isambard Kingdom Brunel on the Great Western Railway. These were followed by the works of Saxby & Farmer Ltd and Westinghouse Brake and Signal Co. Ltd.

Ernest Walls, in *The Bristol Avon*, wrote of coming upon Lacock, from Chippenham past Lackham, 'through meadows thick with buttercups' along a path 'that follows the lazy river's meanderings'. The author observed that the first sight of the abbey was across the breadth of the river and that it was 'as fair a scene as you will gaze upon this side of Jordan'.

Lacock Abbey was founded by Ela, Countess of Salisbury, in 1232, in memory of her husband, William de Longespee, the illegitimate son of Henry II. Ela became the first abbess of the Augustinian nuns at Lacock and endowed the abbey with land, which provided an income from wool during medieval times. The abbey was suppressed in 1539, at the Dissolution of the Monasteries, and the estate was purchased by Sir William Sharington. Although the abbey church was destroyed, much of the medieval building was retained as the property was converted into a residence. Among the early work remaining is the sacristy, warming room and chapter house, the latter opening on to the 15th-century cloisters. A feature of Sharington's work is the distinctive octagonal tower, which was added at the south-east corner of the cloisters.

During medieval times, Lacock was involved in the wool trade and the village prospered. Some of the timber-framed houses date from the 14th century or earlier, while there are stone-built cottages dating from the 17th century and buildings with 18th-century brick facades. In monastic times, the people of Lacock were tenants of the abbey and the village remained in the possession of the new owners of the abbey, the Sharingtons and the Talbots who came after them. In 1944, Miss Matilda Talbot gave her property in Lacock to the National Trust and the village remains unspoiled.

A member of the Talbot family, who made Lacock famous for something other than its abbey and charming village, was William Henry Fox Talbot. A pioneer of photography, his experiments at Lacock Abbey, in the 1830s, led to the production, in 1835, of a photographic negative of the oriel window in the abbey's South Gallery. Standing by the gates to Lacock Abbey is a converted barn, housing the Fox Talbot Museum, which contains a record of the photographic achievements of this early photographer.

In past times, Melksham was associated with the woollen trade. Most of the Melksham tradesmen listed in *Bailey's Western and Midland Directory* of 1783 were clothiers. They included James Bulgin, Lidyards, Bulgin and Phillips, Newman and Collett, Benjamin Webb and Thomas Whitaker. Joseph Yerbury was listed as being 'Clothier and Manufacturer of Ladies Cloths and Cassimeers'. In 1791, *The Universal British Directory of Trade, Commerce and Manufacture* stated, 'The town is noted for its manufacture of superfine cloths and kerseymeres.' By the late 19th century, when the woollen industry had declined, Melksham's industries included the manufacture of ropes, sacking, haircloths, india-rubber and cocoanut [*sic*] fibre.

The Wilts & Berks Canal passed to the east of Melksham and, for a time, the town benefited from Somerset coal, agricultural produce and other local materials, which were transported along it. There was a period of prosperity up to the 1840s, but the coming of the railways led to the canal's decline and its abandonment. Another venture, which didn't prosper, involved the saline and chalybeate springs, found near the town in the 18th century, and another saline spring, which was located in 1816. The latter discovery led to efforts to turn Melksham into a spa town. *Kelly's Directory of Wiltshire* of 1920 noted that 'every accommodation for visitors was provided, including a pump room, hot and cold baths, a handsome crescent and an agreeable promenade'. However, lack of patronage brought about the failure of the scheme.

From Melksham, the River Avon flows in a south-westerly direction towards Staverton, passing under the pack-horse bridge near the village of Whaddon, which has a little church dating from Norman times. Dedicated to St Paul, Staverton's church, like Whaddon's, is near the river. A cloth mill was once by the riverside at Staverton. Just over a century ago this was turned into a large factory producing condensed milk, which was operated by the Anglo-Swiss Condensed Milk Company. Later, under Nestlé, besides condensed milk, the factory made other products such as yoghurt and special desserts and mousses.

The Kennet & Avon Canal runs through the parish of Staverton separating the town of Trowbridge from the river. This waterway was constructed in three sections. The Kennet Navigation, from Reading to Newbury, was built between 1718 and 1723, while work on the Bristol Avon Navigation, between Bath and Bristol, took place between 1724 and 1727. The middle section of the waterway, from Newbury to Bath, was completed in 1810, thus opening up a route from London to Bristol by water. However, after the arrival of the railways, trade on the canal declined. By the mid-20th century, the canal was in such a poor state of repair that it eventually closed as a through route. Restoration of the waterway took place during the second half of the 20th century. The reopening of the route, from Reading to Bristol, was commemorated on 8 August 1990 when Queen Elizabeth II reopened the flight of 29 locks at Caen Hill, Devizes.

Bradford Wharf, on the Kennet & Avon Canal at Bradford-on-Avon, must have been a busy place in the heyday of the canals. Not only was it on the route from London to Bristol, but it was near the junction with the Wilts & Berks Canal at Semington and that of the Somersetshire Coal Canal at Dundas Aqueduct. Goods handled at the wharf included coal, stone, timber and various foodstuffs. There was a gauging dock here, which was used to determine the weight of the cargoes the canal boats were carrying in order to calculate tolls. The wharfinger, who managed the wharf for the Kennet & Avon Canal Company, lived in a house by the lock and the lock keeper's cottage was nearby.

Part of the picturesque town of Bradford-on-Avon rises steeply from the north bank of the river, in a delightful medley of fine stone-built houses and narrow streets.

Like other towns along the River Avon, it was once involved in the woollen trade and became a thriving centre for the industry. In the 17th century Dutch spinners, who were brought into the town, showed the workers new methods. During the prosperous times, the town expanded. *Bailey's Western and Midland Directory* of 1783 listed the Bradford clothiers as John Baskerville, Samuel Bailward, Hart, Moggridge & Co., Robert Halliday, Francis Hill, Thomas Joyce, Thomas Jotham, John Jotham and Joseph and Stephen Phelps. Superfine Clothiers were George Bethell, George Head and Cam, Hillier and Bush.

In 1791, the *Universal British Directory of Trade, Commerce and Manufacture* stated:

> Although it be a town of no very large extent yet it is of considerable importance in the commercial world; great quantities of the finest broadcloths being manufactured here which are eminent for the finest mixtures as the water of the river on which it stands are remarkably qualified for dying the best colours.

As in other towns concerned with the woollen trade, clothiers used to give out wool to be spun and woven by the woollen workers in their own homes. However, trouble loomed when new machinery was introduced, which led to loss of this type of work. In 1791, there was a riot at the residence of clothier, Joseph Phelps, to which there was an adjoining factory. A wooden scribbling machine, used to prepare the wool for spinning, was pulled to the bridge and set alight. By the early 19th century there were 30 woollen manufacturers in the town, but later in this century the woollen trade declined.

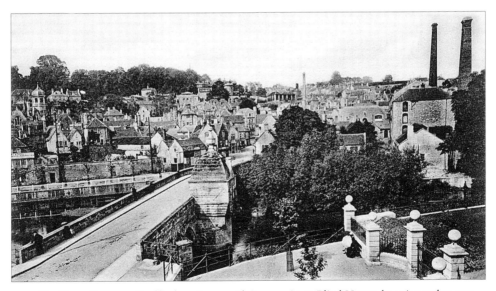

4 The Town Bridge at Bradford-on-Avon, with its prominent Blind House, has nine arches, two of which date from the 13th century. These two early arches are ribbed and pointed, while the others are semicircular in shape. This old postcard view, dating from the early 1900s, shows the town rising on the hill above the river and the tall chimneys of some of Bradford's mills.

In the mid-19th century, a rubber industry was established in deserted mills along the River Avon, which produced waterproof clothing, initially, and then rubber products for railways. Stephen Moulton, the founder of the rubber works, purchased Kingston Mills and nearby Kingston House in 1848. The latter, a late 16th-century mansion, which once belonged to the Dukes of Kingston, was in a dilapidated state at the time of purchase, but was extensively restored. It became renowned at the Paris Exhibition in 1900, where its south front, having been selected as a typical model of its style and period, was recreated for the English pavilion.

Bradford-on-Avon is famous for its unique Saxon church, which is dedicated to St Laurence. The 12th-century monk, William of Malmesbury, wrote that the little church was said to have been built by Aldhelm, Abbot of Malmesbury Abbey, who later became Bishop of Sherborne. However, the style of building of the Saxon church indicates that it may have been erected in the late 10th or early 11th century. Perhaps it was constructed over the foundations of an earlier church. Over the centuries, the building fell into disuse as a place of worship and, by the mid-19th century, the premises were a school. When some work was being done on the building, two angels, carved in stone, were revealed above what was later found to be the chancel arch. This revelation resulted in the vicar of Bradford's Holy Trinity Church, the Rev. W.H. Jones, making another discovery. Looking down on the town from a height, he observed that the roofs of the ancient stone building appeared to have the outline of a chancel, nave and porch of a church. Some years later, after a trust had been formed, the building was restored and a cottage, attached to the church, removed. The vicar wrote *An Account of the Saxon Church of St Laurence* and also a history and description of Bradford-on-Avon, which was annotated and brought up to date by John Beddoe in 1907.

Leaving Bradford-on-Avon, both canal and river head westwards through wooded scenery in a steep-sided valley. At Avoncliff, the canal makes a sharp turn to the right and is carried over the river on the three-arched Avoncliff Aqueduct. Built by John Rennie, between 1796 and 1798, the aqueduct is about 110yds long and is in a delightful location. The *Cross Guns* is thought to date from the 16th century, though a fireplace at this inn may be even earlier. Canal boatmen formerly used the pub for both drinking and for stabling their boat horses overnight. Mill workers, in the past, frequented the pub, too. At one time, part of their pay was in tokens issued by a mill owner who was also the proprietor of the inn. Fulling mills were on the Winsley and the Westwood side of the river in the 18th century. These mills were later used as flock mills. Other mills involved in the woollen industry were at nearby Freshford, on both sides of the River Frome. This river joins the River Avon a little way downstream of Avoncliff Aqueduct.

The Limpley Stoke Valley is the name used, in the locality, for the Avon valley from the village of Limpley Stoke to where it broadens out between the villages of Bathford and Bathampton. Extending along the Avon for around three miles, its beautiful scenery is very attractive to visitors. In the late 19th and early 20th centuries, many visitors came to stay at the West of England Hydropathic Establishment, a

5   A view of the Limpley Stoke Valley showing the railway and the River Avon side by side. In the background is Dundas Aqueduct, which carries the Kennet & Avon Canal across the river. The mill at Limpley Stoke is on the right and the Hydro is in the foreground. The bridge across the Avon at Limpley Stoke is in the centre of the picture.

health resort set in its own grounds and overlooking the river. Patients suffering from indigestion, gout, rheumatism, want of sleep, debility or depression of spirits could be accommodated, but those suffering from infectious diseases or unsound mind or who were otherwise unsuitable were not admitted. Guests staying at the Hydro might arrive by train as there was a station at Limpley Stoke on the Bath and Salisbury Branch of the Great Western Railway.

A bridge on three arches crosses the River Avon at Limpley Stoke and another takes the same road to Winsley over the canal. The river flows past Conkwell Wood, on its right bank, to Dundas Aqueduct, which carries the Kennet & Avon Canal over the valley. Built by John Rennie, in 1804, this three-arched aqueduct, in its beautiful setting, is one of the renowned features of the canal. At Dundas is the junction of the Kennet & Avon Canal with the Somersetshire Coal Canal. The latter, as its name implies, was constructed to carry coal from the Somerset coalfield. From the junction, the coal could be transported northwards then westwards, by water, to Bath or eastwards across the aqueduct into Wiltshire. The Somersetshire Coal Canal was abandoned in 1904 after the railways took away the coal trade from the waterways. However, a short stretch of this canal is still open at Dundas and provides moorings for narrowboats and cruisers.

Downstream from Dundas Aqueduct, there are more wooded slopes on either side of the valley. The river flows past Claverton Wood, on its left bank, and Warleigh Wood on its right bank. Claverton is known for the Claverton Pumping Station, which was designed by John Rennie and built to supply water to the nine-mile stretch of canal between Bradford-on-Avon and Bath. Originally, a large waterwheel, powered by the River Avon, was used to drive the pumping machinery. The waterwheel, beam engines and pumps were restored to full working order by the Kennet and Avon Trust during the late 1960s and early 1970s and the pumping station was reopened in 1978. Another feature of Claverton is the American Museum in Claverton Manor, which is situated high above the village and river with splendid views of the valley. The museum displays American life from colonial times to the 19th century and a particular attraction is the American quilt collection.

6   The flight of six locks, at Widcombe, takes the Kennet & Avon Canal down to join the River Avon at Bath. The locks were completed in 1810, but they sometimes suffered from a shortage of water at which time restrictions were imposed. This Edwardian view of one of the locks shows the tall spire of St Matthew's Church, Widcombe, in the background.

Bathford, downstream of Claverton, is on the opposite side of the river. Its original name is said to have been Forde, indicating a ford across the river, a name by which it was known until the 17th century. In 1791, in *The History and Antiquities of the County of Somerset*, the Rev. John Collinson observed that the situation of Bathford was 'exceedingly pleasant' as it was 'on an eminence at the western declavity of the point of a bold hill, called Farley-Down, which rises behind it to the height of nearly seven hundred feet'. The author remarked that this formed a 'picturesque object' as it was 'so diversified with wild rocks, stone quarries, and irregular patches of wood'. Stone quarrying took place on the opposite side of the river, too, on the downs above Bathampton. Niall Allsop, in *The Kennet & Avon Canal* (1999), noted that this stone was used in the construction of the Kennet & Avon Canal and carried down to the canal at Hampton Quarry Wharf via a tramroad.

After Bathford, the river curves past Batheaston, a village on the road from London to Bath. Its parish church of St John the Baptist has a large pinnacled tower and is situated at North End, where, according to Nikolaus Pevsner, 'the most interesting houses' are located. One of these, Eagle House, was built by the renowned Bath architect, John Wood the elder, in 1772. A toll bridge connects Batheaston with the village of Bathampton. Near the bridge is Bathampton Mill, formerly a flour mill. During the 20th century, the mill was used as tea gardens and it is now a hotel. Bathampton's early 18th-century Manor House, which once belonged to the Allen family, has also undergone a change in use and has been converted to a residential home for the elderly. Dedicated to St Nicholas, the village church, too, has seen its share of change over the last three centuries, being mostly rebuilt by Ralph Allen in the mid-18th century and altered during Victorian times. The church is close to the Kennet & Avon Canal, which is crossed by a bridge with a horseshoe arch. Nearby is the canalside *George Inn*, where, it is said, a Frenchman, the loser in the country's last legal duel, was carried before he died.

From Bathampton, the River Avon flows into Bath past Walcot and Bathwick, while the Kennet & Avon Canal makes its way into Bath, on the south side of the city, past Sydney Gardens. Sydney Wharf would, no doubt, have been lively in the heyday of the canal. In 1822, *Pigot & Co.'s Directory* noted that Euclid Shaw & Co. provided conveyance, by water, from Sydney Wharf to London, weekly, and to Bristol on a Tuesday. At this time, John Peacock ran a boat to Bristol and Devizes, weekly, from the same wharf. The canal passes down a flight of six locks at Widcombe to join the River Avon. Five of these locks are around nine feet deep, but Bath Deep Lock, the fifth lock in the flight, is 19ft 5in deep. Two locks were made into one when this part of the canal was restored in 1976. The junction of the canal and river is at Bath Bottom Lock, on the opposite side of the river from Bath railway station.

Guidebooks and directories of Bath, written in the 18th and 19th centuries, pay little attention to the River Avon at Bath, preferring to dwell on the fine architecture of the city, its hot springs and baths and the fashionable company who came as visitors. A brief reference to the river, in *The Bath and Bristol Guide* of 1755, includes the information that barges, which chiefly belonged to Mr Bradley, went occasionally from Bath and that, for freight, customers had to agree at his house on the 'Key'. This guidebook also noted: 'Messrs. *Palmer, Moore* and *Cole*, have Two good Barges, for the carrying of Goods, &c. from their Ware-House on *Bath Key*, to the *Bridgewater Slip* on the *Back, Bristol*.' By 1791, according to the Rev. John Collinson, the number of barges employed on the river, to and from Bristol, was nine and their burden was on average 30 tons each.

The Rev. John Collinson, in *The History and Antiquities of the County of Somerset*, gave this description of the situation of Bath:

> It stands in a narrow valley, bounded on the north, east, south and southwest by lofty hills, forming a very pleasant natural amphitheatre, and affording the city a double advantage, a barrier against the winds, and fountains of the purest water. This valley runs nearly from northeast to northwest, being incurvated in its centre by the swelling ridge of Lansdown-hill, which is its chief boundary towards the north. On the northwest side, it widens, and gradually opens into a plain, divided into rich meads and pastures, and watered by the River Avon (the Antona of Tacitus) which, leaving the city on its northern banks, hence winds its way to Keynsham, and the port of Bristol.

When thoughts turn to the River Avon at Bath, the elegant Pulteney Bridge, with its three arches and small shops on either side, may come to mind. This was designed by Robert Adam and completed in 1773. Before the bridge was built, access to Bathwick from the city was by ferry. This ferry and the quay from where the boats crossed was mentioned by the Bath architect, John Wood, in *An Essay towards a Description of Bath* (1749):

> STALL BOAT QUAY, commonly called the *Boat Stall*, ... Was formerly a broad, spacious Walk, upon that Part of the Shore of the *Avon* which is under the City Wall between the North and East Gates; at the South End of which there was antiently a Cross for the Sale of our River Fish; with a Ducking-Stool near it, for the Punishment of Disorderly Women: And at the North End there is a Ferry, for a Communication between the City and the Villages of *Bathwick* and *Hamton*. From the little Boats kept here, on this Occasion, as well as for the Use of the Fishermen, called *Stall-Boats*, this *Quay* had its name.

A less-well-known bridge may be Widcombe Footbridge, which opened in 1863 and gave residents, on the south side of the river, easy access to the railway station. This bridge was known as the Ha'penny Bridge as it was a toll bridge with the toll-house at the Widcombe end. On 7 June 1877, hundreds of people, who had just arrived by train, converged at the bridge to cross to the show ground of the Bath and West of England Agriculture Society, which was celebrating its centenary. As there

7   The River Avon at Bath looking downstream from Churchill Bridge, 2005. In the early 20th century, Bath's riverside along Lower Bristol Road had a number of industrial premises. These included the Camden steam flour mills of James Collins & Sons, Charles Bayer & Co., corset manufacturers and Stothert and Pitt Ltd, engineers.

was only one toll-collector, progress across the bridge was slow. It was estimated that there were between two and three hundred people on the bridge when it started to collapse. Fortunately, many were able to get off the bridge before it fell into the water. Eight people were killed in the catastrophe and about fifty were injured.

There had been a bridge at the site of Bath's Old Bridge since at least the mid-14th century. In *An Essay towards a Description of Bath*, John Wood stated:

> *Saint Laurence's Bridge* makes a Passage over the River *Avon*, for joining *Horse Street* to *Haulway*: And the Structure consists of five Apertures, covered with Semi-Circular Arches: The Top of the Bridge is Eleven Feet six Inches broad over the Arches; but much wider over the Butments; and the Buildings fronting it are the small Chapel of Saint *Laurence*, elevated over one of the Piers, and four dwelling Houses erected on the Banks of the River, by the side of the Butments of the Bridge. The Narrowness of this Bridge is now become a publick Nuisance.

In 1754, the bridge was rebuilt, while in 1847 it was widened, the old stone parapet was removed and a pierced iron parapet was added. The Old Bridge was a problem during times of flood as debris would pile up in its arches, restricting the flow of water and diverting it over the banks of the river. After floods in 1823, the civil engineer, Thomas Telford, was asked for help to find a suitable flood defence scheme. Among his recommendations was the proposal to replace the Old Bridge by a single-span structure. This was not acceptable because of the high costs involved, which included other plans to tame the floods. Eventually, in 1964, the Old Bridge was taken down. It was replaced by Southgate Footbridge and the single-span Southgate Bridge. The latter, 40yds downstream of the site of the Old Bridge, was renamed Churchill Bridge after the death of Sir Winston Churchill in 1965.

According to John Wood, the 'Key', on the north shore of the River Avon and on the west side of St Laurence's Bridge, was made in 1729 'for the Purpose of landing Goods brought to the City by Water'. John Wood gave its measurements as 480ft in length and 97ft in breadth. No doubt, in the late 18th and early 19th centuries, the riverside downstream of Old Bridge would have been bustling at times. In *The New History, Survey and Description of the City and Suburbs of Bristol or Complete Guide* (1794), published by William Matthews, it was observed:

> On the western side of this Bridge is the Quay of Bath, from whence the River is navigable to Bristol, so that Bath is a proper inland Port. Barges that have one mast and sail, and carry from 60 to 80 Tons, bring heavy goods from Bristol, iron, copper, wine, deals and many other articles, and generally return laden with large blocks of Freestone ...

Stone for building was in great demand in the early 18th century. Ralph Allen, the owner of quarries at Combe Down, had a railway constructed from his quarries down to a wharf on the Widcombe side of the River Avon upstream of the Old Bridge. This railway went past his mansion, Prior Park, and was such an innovation that many people came to view the wooden waggons, loaded with stone, descending. At Allen's Wharf, the stone was craned into barges and then carried down the Avon to Bristol from where it could be transported to other parts of the country.

The Quay downstream of the Old Bridge was later referred to as Broad Quay. In 1822, conveyance by water, to London and Bristol, was undertaken twice a week by Betts and Drewe from Broad Quay, while Charles Thomas of Broad Quay sent boats to Bristol twice a week. *Pigot & Co.'s Directory* of 1822 also noted that goods were sent weekly to Bristol and forwarded to all parts of the north by Thomas Jorden of Norfolk Quay, Bath. However, *Pigot & Co.'s Directory* of 1830 and 1844 made no reference to conveyance by water from Broad Quay. Then, the wharves handling goods in Bath were on the Kennet & Avon Canal.

The River Avon navigation with its six locks, between Bath and Hanham Mills, was constructed between 1724 and 1727 under the supervision of the engineer, John Hore. In *An Essay towards a Description of Bath*, John Wood described the first cargo conveyed along the waterway on 15 December 1727: 'upon that Day the first Barge was brought up to the City, laden with Deal-Boards, Pig-Lead, and Meal.' The toll on the River Avon at this time for the carrying of coal was 'fifteen Pence for every Tun of four and twenty Bushels'. Other cargoes for which tolls were charged on the new navigation included stone, slate, tiles, gravel, sand, bricks, timber, boards, wine, cider, oil, grain, hay, straw and wool. Passengers were charged a toll of 3d. for every person.

According to a Bristol publication, *Farley's Newspaper*, passengers were being carried on the River Avon even before the navigation was completed. In the issue dated 2 September 1727, an accident was recorded concerning 'the new Passage Boat between Bristol and Twerton'. The following year, a royal passenger used the new waterway for travel. Princess Amelia, the daughter of George II, who was at Bath, paid a visit to Bristol on 9 May 1728 on the invitation of the Common Council. She landed at Countess-slip (Counterslip) on Temple Back where she was received by the Mayor and Aldermen in their scarlet robes. In the afternoon, she returned to Bath by water.

The Bath and Bristol Guide of 1755 noted, '*Wherries* for Pleasuring, and for *Bristol*, may be had of Mr. *Tomkins*, at the *Vernon-Inn*, near the Bridge, BATH.' However, by the late 19th century, it would seem that a pleasure boat on the river was likely to be something of an event, at least in the poorer quarters on the riverside. In the novel, *The Strange Adventures of a House-Boat* (1889), William Black remarked:

> The approach to the beautiful Queen of the West, by the valley of the Avon, is disappointing in the extreme; indeed, the slums here are about as bad as those of the Totterdown suburb of Bristol. Our appearance in these squalid outskirts was the signal for a mighty flutter of excitement; from all quarters there came rushing a multitude of ragged mudlarks – between five and fifteen their ages seemed for the most part to range – not one of whom, as far as we could see, was possessed of cap or bonnet; and these formed our ever-increasing escort as we slowly passed along the muddy waters. Nor was the general perturbation confined to those on foot; everywhere windows were thrown open, and dishevelled heads thrust out; there were calls from this house to that; and echoing answers from below. When at last we stopped at one of the quays – amid cranes, and piles of wood, and coal, and what not – the crowd grew greater than ever.

8 Weston Lock, the first lock downstream on the River Avon, is encountered on the edge of Bath. Having a fall of 9ft 3in, it is the deepest of the six locks between Bath and Hanham.

In the 1890s, one of the businesses at Bath's Broad Quay was that of J.A. Bladwell & Co., slate importers and general builders' merchants. Their warehouses were mostly two storeys high and contained a large assortment of goods including large quantities of slate slabs imported directly from the quarries of Penrhyn. On the site, there were sawing and planing mills, operated by steam power, which could produce every kind of slatework. As there was stabling and cart accommodation on the premises, the firm distributed its goods by road as well as by river or the Great Western and Midland Railways.

At this time, further down the river, at Sydenham Wharf, Lower Bristol Road, Bath Stone Works was run by Henry W. Bladwell. His spacious stoneyard, on the banks of the river, had sheds equipped with the appliances for the dressing and moulding of Bath stone by skilled workmen. Bath stone, for churches and public buildings, was a speciality of these works, which had provided stone for buildings in Cambridge, Newcastle-upon-Tyne and Carlisle as well as for Bath.

Downstream of Bath, the river enters Weston Cut, a channel leading to Weston Lock. When this cut was excavated an island was made. The island is often referred to as Weston Island. However, Niall Allsop, in *Images of the Kennet & Avon* (1987), noted that it became known as Dutch Island after the nationality of the owner of the brass mill, which was set up on the river side of the island in the 18th century. It appears that there was once a distinct Dutch community in the neighbourhood. In the 19th century, there was a tall cloth mill alongside Weston Lock, but the mill no longer exists.

Concerning the river in this vicinity, at the end of the 18th century, William Matthews' *New History of Bristol* stated:

> The River, though quite fresh, is deep, of a good width, beautifully winds on towards Bristol, in an exquisitely delightful and happy Vale, between verdant hills and rural villages; and swarms with fine fishes, trout, roche, dace, perch, eels and others: about 2 miles and a half from Bath, it runs under a noble Bridge of Stone of one arch, that for height and expansion seems to rival the Rialto at Venice. A little farther on, is a lofty eminence, beautifully impending over its northern bank, on which are pleasantly situated, the elegant Mansion and Park of Sir Caesar Hawkins, Bart. Seven miles from Bristol, between Saltford and Bitton, it becomes the boundary between Glocestershire [*sic*] and Somerset, and so continues till it falls into the Bristol Channel.

The 'noble Bridge of Stone' was New Bridge. Altered since its original construction, it is an unusual bridge with two cylindrical openings in its single arch and a number of flood arches on each side. Kelston Park is the name of the mansion on the river's right bank. A striking landmark of this vicinity is tree-topped Kelston Round Hill, known to locals as Kelston Tump. Kelston, a village on the upper road from Bath to Bristol, gives its name to Kelston Lock, though the latter is actually nearer Saltford then Kelston.

A century and more ago, people came to Saltford seeking relaxation on the river and riverside. Visitors still do so today. In 1906, Clifton Rowing Club had a membership of 80 at its picturesque boathouse. Joseph Withey built a boat hiring station above Kelston Lock, on the Saltford side of the river, in the 1890s. In the next decade, a rival establishment was set up by George Sheppard. These boathouses enjoyed some success as the visitors who hired their craft were able to take advantage of boating on a mile-long straight stretch known as the Long Reach.

Saltford's 18th-century brass mill, situated near Kelston Lock, was originally a fulling mill. It was among a number of brass mills, which were set up when the centre of the area's brass-making industry moved upriver from Baptist Mills, on the River Frome, at Bristol. Brass pans were among the goods shipped out from Bristol to Africa in the days of the slave trade. Neptune Pans were among the different sorts of pans made at Saltford and exported to West Africa. Sea water was evaporated in these very shallow pans, which resulted in the production of sea salt.

There was once a passenger ferry near Saltford's brass mill. *Kelly's Directory of Somersetshire* of 1895 lists Charles Gregory as ferryman, but it was his wife, Hannah, who worked the ferry boat. In past times, a horse ferry was on the river above Saltford Lock as here the towing path changed sides. The boat for carrying the horses was flat-bottomed. The ferry was worked by pulling the boat across the river on a chain, which was threaded through the boat and attached to the banks on either side. This was the second horse ferry coming downriver. The first was upriver, opposite Kelston Park, while a third horse ferry was downstream of Swineford Lock.

Just over a decade after the navigation between Bath and Bristol had opened, Saltford Lock was the scene of some disturbance over the transport of coal by water. John Wood, in *An Essay towards a Description of Bath*, commented:

> Coal from *Shropshire* became one of the chief Commodities brought to the City by Water; which tho' not so good in General as the Coal raised in our own Neighbourhood, yet it is preferable to the greatest Part for Chamber Fires; and the Company, who frequent the City, have used it accordingly. This soon stirred up our Colliers to threaten to destroy the Locks of the River, to stop this Branch of Trade.

An Act of Parliament subsequently made the destruction, after 15 May 1735, of 'any Lock, Sluice, Flood-Gate, or any other Works on any Navigable River, erected, or to be erected by Authority of Parliament', an offence punishable by death. However, this didn't stop Saltford Lock being almost destroyed by saboteurs in 1738. The proprietors of the navigation offered 'a Reward of Twenty Pounds, for the Discovery of every Person concerned in the Outrage committed on their Work'. This preserved the locks from any further disturbance and the coal trade was still carried on along the navigation.

The *Jolly Sailor*, adjacent to Saltford Lock, was much frequented by the boat crews and its stables were used for their horses. Niall Allsop, in *Images of the Kennet & Avon*, recounted the custom of new boatmen marking the occasion of becoming familiar with the river by pushing a red-hot poker into the wooden surround of the inn's fireplace. The earliest-known landlord of the *Jolly Sailor* is said to be Francis Hunt who kept the inn for a number of years from the mid-18th century.

Not far downstream is Swineford Lock, the fourth lock on the river. The mill near the lock was originally a fulling and tucking mill, but later became one of the mills involved in the brass and copper industry. Swineford is connected with the legend of Bladud, a swineherd whose leprosy had been caught by the animals he was tending. It is said that, after driving his pigs across a shallow place on the Avon, the location became known as Swineford. The story continues with the pigs rushing downhill and wallowing in a spot where warm springs issuing from the ground made a muddy morass. By doing this, the pigs were cured of their disease and Bladud, on observing the effect, bathed at the same place and was healed, too. This tale is also part of the folklore of Bath as the place with the healing waters eventually became Bath Spa.

A little way downstream of Swineford Lock, Bitton Railway Bridge, which was once used by trains on the former Mangotsfield to Bath Green Park branch of the Midland Railway, now carries a cycle route, the Bristol and Bath Railway Path and the track of the Avon Valley Railway. Return train trips aboard a steam train can be taken, mainly during the summer months, on the six-mile-long Avon Valley Railway line. This preserved railway is based at nearby Bitton station. The parish of Bitton stretches along the north bank of the Avon, while the village of the same name stands by a tributary, the River Boyd, which once powered Bitton's paper mill. Bitton, on the edge of the ancient Kingswood Forest, was also in the Gloucestershire coalfield and, in times past, many inhabitants of the parish were engaged in coal mining. The neighbourhood was infamous for the unruliness of the Kingswood colliers and the parish of Bitton was renowned for the Cock Road Gang, a notorious band of robbers who operated in the area during the early 19th century. When caught, some of these criminals were hung and others transported.

The town of Keynsham, on the south bank of the River Avon, stands near the confluence of the River Chew with the River Avon. It was formerly famous for its abbey, which was founded by William, Earl of Gloucester *c*.1170. Traditionally, Keynsham's name is said to have originated from St Keyna, the daughter of a Welsh chief, who crossed over the Severn and made her way up the Avon seeking a quiet religious life away from suitors for her hand in marriage. A local chief gave her land, but it was swarming with snakes. St Keyna dealt with them by turning them into stone with her prayers. Interestingly, the area around Keynsham is known for fossils called ammonites, which resemble a coiled snake. However, another interpretation of the town's name is that it is derived from the British tribe called the Cangi.

In the 18th century, Keynsham was also spelt Canesham or Cainsham. John Stuckey, in *A compleat history of Somersetshire* (1742), observed, 'It seems to be a foggy smoky place, because it is proverbially called Smoky-Canesham.' At this time, Keynsham was famed for elvers, which came upriver on the spring tides. John Stuckey noted that here the river was 'covered over and coloured black, with millions of little eels, scarce as big as a goose quill'. The elvers were caught in great numbers with small nets and then boiled and made into small cakes. These elver cakes were sold at Bath and Bristol, then fried and eaten with butter.

9 The Harford and Bristol Brass Company began making brass alongside the River Avon at Keynsham in 1706. Brass workers from the Dutch-German border, near Aachen, were recruited to work in the riverside brass mill. Among these workers was a family called Ollis who stayed in the neighbourhood for over two centuries. When the brass mill closed down in 1927, the foreman was a member of this family. This view of part of the brass mill dates from the early years of the 20th century.

Keynsham's industries in the 18th century included malting and brass making. The Avon and Chew Mills produced goods such as wire and battery wares. The mill on the River Avon continued as a brass works until 1927, but the works on the River Chew eventually became mills, which were used to crush ochre to be used in the manufacture of paint. Another Keynsham industry was the Polysulphin Soap Works. This was established on the Avon, in the late 19th century, upstream from the brass works. Materials for the soap works, such as drums of oil and soda ash, were brought up the River Avon from Avonmouth and Bristol.

Downstream of Keynsham Lock are the striking red-brick buildings of the chocolate factory, known as Somerdale, which formerly belonged to the firm, J.S. Fry & Sons. This company, for many years one of the biggest employers in Bristol, moved their business from the city to Somerdale for a variety of reasons. One was that raw materials could be transported to the new factory from Avonmouth Docks and from Bristol by water. Originally built in the 1920s, with later additions in 1933 and 1960, the factory, now operated by Cadbury Schweppes, is an imposing sight on the riverside. Passing the works, the Avon makes a loop around Keynsham Hams before taking a sharp bend to the right on its approach to Hanham Lock. The latter is numbered as the first lock on the Kennet & Avon Canal. Above the lock, the navigation is under the authority of British Waterways. Below the lock, the River Avon is under the jurisdiction of Bristol City Council and the river is tidal.

After Hanham Lock, the steep-sided wooded valley is thought by some to rival the scenery of the Thames. This was the opinion of Cyril Herbert Smith who wrote about a journey down the Avon in *Through the Kennet and Avon Canal by Motor Boat in 1928* (1929). He noted that the river ran in a 'deep gorge' with the left bank covered in woods right down to the water's edge and the right bank partly wooded and partly showing red sandstone rocks. The scenery was so attractive that, although he and his wife meant to moor their boat for the night below Hanham Lock, they couldn't resist travelling for a further two and a half miles downstream to see what was around each bend.

At Conham, the river makes a horseshoe bend. In the past, Conham Ferry was well-used by people crossing between the Gloucestershire and Somerset sides of the river. Bees' Tea Gardens, by the ferry and on the Somerset bank, was established in the mid-19th century and continues to attract visitors, some of whom take a cruise upriver from Bristol. The picturesque location also became popular with rowers, the Bristol Ariel Rowing Club having set up their headquarters along this reach of the river in 1900, when the club moved from Bristol Bridge. In 1928, Cyril Herbert Smith was permitted to use a mooring here for several days. He commented on going up the zigzag path, through the woods to the club's entrance and finding it strange that the quiet boathouse was so close to what was fast becoming a suburb of Bristol and to the busy commercial city itself.

Built in the late 17th century, there was once a copper works at Conham, which was later taken over by the Bristol Brass Company. During the 18th century, this company had many furnaces in Crews Hole, an industrial area downriver from

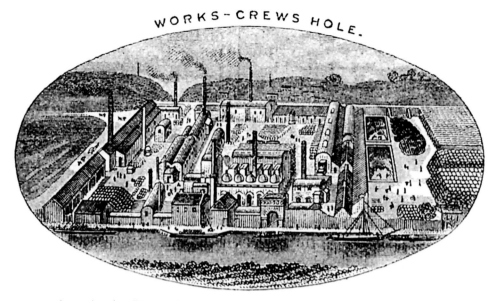

10   The works of William Butler & Co., Tar, Rosin and Oil Distillers, at Crews Hole, 1893.

Conham. There are several opinions on how Crews Hole obtained its unusual name. One theory is that the name is derived from the surname of a family who owned land in the vicinity. Another view is that the name is derived from the crews of ships who took shelter upriver when press gangs were roaming Bristol.

In times past, Crews Hole was well known for the riverside works operated by William Butler & Co., Tar, Rosin and Oil Distillers. The firm was founded by William Butler in 1843. Besides the large manufactory at Crews Hole, it had another works at Upper Parting, Gloucester. In the 1890s, the company employed a small fleet, comprising six lighters and a steam tug at Bristol and three lighters at Gloucester. Using this water transport, they could ship goods from their works at Crews Hole and deliver them either to the railway yards in Bristol or alongside coasting vessels or ships bound for foreign ports, which were in the docks. Return cargoes were raw materials for distillation and freights of turpentine and rosin, which were imported in great quantities by the firm. At this time, four trows were also owned by the company. These were used to carry the firm's products to ports in South Wales. A coasting steamer, the *Clifton Grove*, delivered tar and creosote to other ports in the country and on the continent.

Firms with works by the river at Crews Hole, in the late 19th and early 20th centuries, were the Bristol Fire Clay Company and the Crown Clay Company. Both of these companies made firebricks though the latter also produced other wares. Downriver from these concerns, the chemical works at Netham was a prominent sight along the river at this time. In 1875, these works manufactured alkali, caustic soda, soda crystals, bleaching powder, sulphuric and muriatic acids, murite of soda and sal ammoniac. Between four and five hundred men were employed there.

Just downstream from Crews Hole, on the opposite side of the river, there was once a chapel at St Anne's, which had been established in the 13th century. Henry VII and his queen, Elizabeth of York, are said to have visited the nearby spring known as St Anne's Well. St Anne's Ferry had also been in existence since medieval times, but this crossing closed in 1957 when a public footbridge replaced it. The site of the chapel became part of St Anne's Board Mill, which started producing carton board in 1915. This was supplied to the neighbouring Mardon's factory where cigarette cartons were manufactured and printed for Bristol's Imperial Tobacco Company. St Anne's Board Mill was also one of the main suppliers of board for cartons and packaging in the country. The large riverside complex, which once used the Avon for transport, was demolished in the early 1980s and the area has been redeveloped for housing.

At Netham, the tidal river flows over Netham Weir into the New Cut, a channel dug in the early 19th century when Bristol's Floating Harbour was constructed. Past Netham Lock, the Feeder Canal takes the navigation through an industrial area into the Floating Harbour. In *The Strange Adventures of a House-Boat*, William Black described the area along the Feeder Canal as a 'most squalid neighbourhood' and mentioned passing through 'malodorous suburbs, that seemed to consist almost exclusively of manufactories'. Works along the Feeder Canal at the turn of the 19th and 20th centuries included the Netham Constructional Steel Works, the Avonside Tannery, manure works, galvanised iron works and soap and candle works.

11   At Netham Lock, the lock gates are left open when the river level is normal. They are closed when high spring tides top nearby Netham Weir.

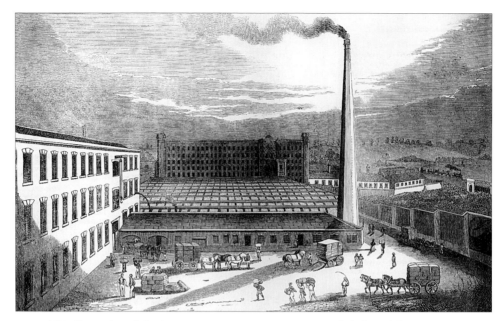

12   This illustration of the Great Western Cotton Factory was included in *Chilcott's Descriptive History of Bristol* (1844), which noted:

> The print annexed shows the mill where the cotton is spun into yarn. The room at the foot of the mill is the weaving room, where about 500 young women are employed in making the yarn spun in the mill into cloth ... In the building to the left, all the looms and a considerable portion of the other machinery are made and repaired.

One of the factories along the canal belonged to the Great Western Cotton Works. In 1837-8, this was established by the association of several of the leading inhabitants of Bristol with J.B. Clarke, an eminent manufacturer of Manchester. By 1851, there were six engines at the cotton factory, four of 80 horse power and two of 20 horse power, which were continually kept working. Then, the establishment generally employed upwards of 1,700 people who were involved in spinning, weaving and bleaching. In 1875, there were 800 looms in the factory's large room, the manufacture being chiefly for the East India and China markets. The works ceased manufacturing cotton in 1925.

William Matthews' *New History of Bristol* described the River Avon's entry into the city, in the late 18th century, before the construction of the Feeder Canal and Bristol's Floating Harbour:

> It enters the eastern suburbs of Bristol, between glass-houses, iron-founderies, distilleries, breweries, and, sugar-houses; goes on to the City, and runs under its last and most eminent Bridge. Here, the Avon is clear and shallow at low water, deep and muddy at high water, but one of the deepest, safest, and most convenient for Navigation, in England. It is 200 feet wide at the Bridge, at high Tides rises from 25 to 30 feet perpendicularly ... often overflows, the Key; has an agreeable effect when full, renders the port very pleasant, and will waft the largest Merchant Ships and even Ships of War up to the Bridge in the heart of the City.

The Anglo-Saxon settlement, which grew up between the two rivers, Avon and Frome, became known as Brigstowe, the place by the bridge. By the 12th century, variations in its name include both Bristow and Bristol and its bridge was probably a wooden structure. In 1247, a new four-arched stone bridge was built. Later, this bridge was renowned for the five-storeyed dwellings built out over its sides. A chapel, which had been erected across the middle of the bridge in 1361, was destroyed by fire in 1642. Nevertheless, even without the chapel, the 19ft-wide passage across the ancient bridge must have been dark with the houses towering on either side of it. The old Bristol Bridge was superseded by a new bridge, which was opened in 1768. Tolls were charged to pay for its erection, but, by 1793, some of the Bristol citizens thought that enough money must have accumulated to cover the cost and that passage across the bridge should now be free. Rioting broke out, during which 11 people were killed and 45 were injured. Eventually, further opposition was avoided when the money required to free the bridge from tolls was raised privately.

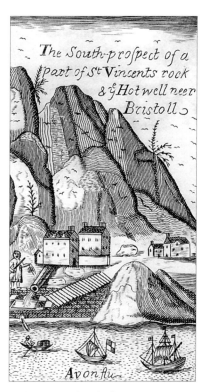

13   Views of old Bristol from Samuel Seyer's *Memoirs both Historical and Topographical of Bristol and its Neighbourhood*, which was published in two volumes in 1821 and 1823. These views had been copied from Millerd's 1673 plan of Bristol. The first shows the large house, which once stood at the corner of Redcliffe Street and old Bristol Bridge. In the middle is a bird's-eye view of old Bristol Bridge. The third depicts St Vincent's Rock with the Hotwell spring flowing out of the river's muddy bank.

In 1794, Bristol Bridge was the only bridge over the River Avon, but there were 13 bridges of stone and four of wood in the city and suburbs over its tributary, the River Frome. The Drawbridge was the lowest bridge on the Frome before its confluence with the Avon. It had two stone arches and a drawbridge, which could be raised to let coasting vessels and Severn trows pass. The next bridge, over the Frome, was St Giles's Bridge at the head of the Quay, known also as the Stone Bridge. Both this bridge and Frome Bridge, just above it, had two stone arches. The other bridges were St John's, Bridewell, Needless, Pithay, Union, Merchant's, Philadelphia, Ellbridge, Penn's and Traitor's bridges, the latter being the first bridge that the Frome encountered when it entered Bristol on the north-eastern side of the city. These were all one-arched stone bridges.

This description of the Quay at Bristol, as it was in 1794, appeared in William Matthews' *New History of Bristol*:

> The Quay of Bristol is towards of a mile in extent or circuit, reaching from St Giles's-bridge down to the mouth of the Froom, and up the Avon to Bristol-bridge; being one uninterrupted spacious Wharf of hewn stone, having sufficient depth of water before it for Ships of the greatest burden and fully laden to come up close to the walls and discharge their cargoes. It has different names, as the head of the Key, Tontine Key, Broad Key, the Gibb, Mud Dock, the Grove and the Back. At this Key, lie safely on a soft bed of mud, a considerable number of Ships, at all times, of the year; which make a pleasing appearance, and the large quantities of different Merchandize seen on the Wharfs, prove the very great Trade of the port of Bristol.

Bristol's importance was built on its trade. A notable Bristol merchant of the 15th century was William Canynges, the younger, who died in 1474. He had owned a fleet of vessels, which traded to ports in foreign countries. On his epitaph, in St Mary Redcliffe Church, he was described as 'ye Richest Marchant of ye town of Bristow'. The inscription mentioned the names of nine of his ships and an unnamed vessel along with their burdens. Besides being renowned as a merchant and as five times Mayor of Bristol, William Canynges was also involved in the rebuilding of the church of St Mary Redcliffe after the fall of its spire in 1445.

New lands were discovered in the West at the end of the 15th century and Bristol merchants were able to expand their commercial interests. John Cabot, who set sail from Bristol in the *Matthew*, is famous for his voyage of discovery across the Atlantic in 1497. However, it is said that men of Bristol sailing westward had already found and discovered the land that Cabot had seen. A great number of expeditions were ventured from Bristol, over the next two hundred years, which brought much prosperity to the city's trade. Edward VI granted the Society of Merchant Venturers a Royal Charter in 1552. The Society controlled, protected and promoted the trade of the city, while all shipping entering and leaving the port came under its jurisdiction.

The African slave trade came into prominence in the late 17th century and proved very lucrative. Three profits could be made on a round voyage. Goods from Bristol were shipped to the African coast where they were exchanged for slaves bound for the plantations of the West Indies. Ships coming back from the West Indies bore sugar, rum and mahogany. In 1794, William Matthews' *New History of Bristol* stated: 'The Ardor for the Trade to Africa for men and women, our fellow creatures and equals, is much abated among the humane and benevolent Merchants of Bristol.' Nevertheless, by 1787, there were still 30 Bristol ships employed in this 'melancholy traffic'.

In the 1790s, there was considerable trade also to Florida, Carolina, Virginia, Maryland, New York, Philadelphia, Newfoundland, Quebec and Nova Scotia. Ships exported Bristol manufactures, which were sent through the continent of North America, and returned laden with tobacco, rice, tar, deer skins, timber, furs, indigo and logwood. Bristol merchants also traded with Holland and Hamburg, sent ships to Norway, the Baltic and Russia for hemp and deals, and imported a great deal of

14   Bristol's first dock scheme involved the cutting of a great trench, into which the River Frome was diverted. This undertaking, along with the making of the Quay, is thought to have taken place in 1247-8 and cost the city £5,000. The channel was 120ft wide and 2,400ft long with a depth of 18ft. The diverted Frome, which formerly joined the River Avon near St Nicholas' Church, now flowed between Canon's Marsh and The Marsh to its junction with the Avon. This engraving, showing ships at Bristol, was published on 1 July 1799 in *The Itinerant: A Selection of Interesting and Picturesque Views, in Great Britain and Ireland.*

fruit, wine and oil from the Mediterranean. Besides foreign goods, home-produced commodities were also conveyed to Bristol by water. William Barrett, in *The History and Antiquities of the City of Bristol* (1789) observed:

> A market is also held on the Back every other Wednesday, where the Welch boats, arriving at spring tides, discharge the produce of their country for sale; fine salt-butter, poultry of all kinds, roasting geese ready for the spit, fruit as apples, pears, &c. The great brewhouses and malthouses, the bakers and cornfactors, are furnished with corn and flour by water carriage from the West Country and the fertile vale of Evesham, and the counties of Hereford, Monmouth and Worcester, which is landed on St. Austin's wharf, at the head of the Quay, out of the trows; or on the Back, where convenient market-houses are built for securing it when landed from the weather, and there exposed to sale every spring tide: – here are also landed great quantities of cyder.

Up to the early 1800s, Bristol with its ancient tidal harbour was the second port in the United Kingdom. However, it was recognised that the formation of a floating harbour, undisturbed by tides, would be an advantage to the sea-faring city. The creation of Bristol's Floating Harbour, which took place between 1803 and 1809, involved the damming of the River Avon at Totterdown, in the east, and at Red Clift House, in the west, to give a two-and-a-half-mile stretch of harbour and around eighty acres of deep water. The work was to the plans of William Jessop by whose name the first entrance locks at Cumberland Basin were known. This undertaking also included the construction of the Feeder Canal to connect the new Floating Harbour with the river at Netham and to provide fresh water to the docks. A new channel for the tidal river, extending from Netham to Rownham, was excavated, a lock being made at Totterdown for light barge traffic, and another leading into Bathurst Basin for ships. In January 1809, the river was diverted into this new bed, which became known as the New Cut. The estimate of the cost of the works had initially been £3,000, but the total cost eventually rose to £6,000.

Despite the creation of the Floating Harbour, during the first half of the 19th century Bristol lost its position as the country's second port. In other ports the rates were reduced on ships, but in Bristol they remained unaltered. John Morgan, in *A Brief Historical Sketch of Bristol with the New Picture of Clifton, and Stranger's Guide* (1851), observed that Bristol had 'dwindled down to a fifth-rate Port'. In 1848, an Act of Parliament transferred the operation and property of the City Docks from the company, which had carried out the construction of the Floating Harbour, to the City of Bristol. That year tonnage rates were reduced. There were great celebrations in Bristol on 15 November 1848, the day when the reduction in port dues took effect. A procession wound through the city, which was decorated for the occasion, and church bells rang.

By the mid-19th century, Bristol's most important foreign trade was still with the West Indies. The exports were materials for building, including great quantities of lime. Other goods exported to the islands were clothing, bottled liquors and implements used in the sugar plantations. Imports from the West Indies included

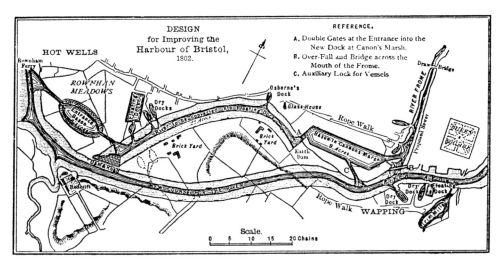

15 William Jessop's original plan for the Floating Harbour included a large basin of nine acres, which was to be dug out at Canon's Marsh. As a great objection to this plan was that it left the River Avon from Prince Street Bridge still tidal, he put forward an improved plan for the Floating Harbour and this was carried out.

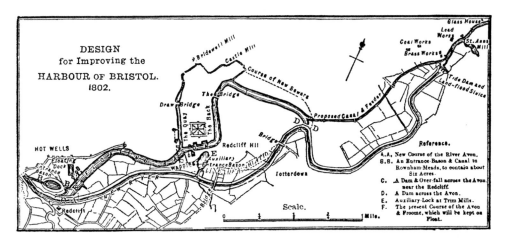

sugar, rum, coffee and cotton. Among the sugar refiners in Bristol, in 1850, were Bernard Vining & Co. at Quay Head, Hier & Stock in Old Market Street and Finzel & Son, Counterslip. The latter was a very large establishment. At this time, the refined sugars produced in Bristol were said to be of superior quality, great quantities being exported to Ireland and a substantial amount to South Wales.

In the 1850s, there was considerable traffic between Bristol and ports in Ireland and South Wales. Some of the coasting vessels to South Wales were operated from Welsh Back, Narrow Quay and the Grove, while those to Ireland were operated from Broad Quay. Among the steam packets, which travelled to both South Wales and Ireland, were those run by Lunell & Co., Broad Quay, while John Jones, Rownham Wharf, sent steam packets to Chepstow, daily.

Charles Frederick Cliffe described the scene at Cumberland Basin in *The Book of South Wales, the Bristol Channel, Monmouthshire, and the Wye* (1847):

> Cumberland Basin: Generally presents an animated scene when the tide is in, as it is the rendezvous of nearly all the steam packets belonging to the port. The great days of departure are Tuesdays and Fridays; and what between the rush of passengers 'outward,' and the arrival of steamers brimful of bipeds and Irish pigs 'inward,' there is always a scramble until the tide turns.

In 1850, besides vessels in the coastal trade, there were craft, which traded from Bristol along the rivers Severn, Wye, Usk, Parrett and Tone and along the Kennet & Avon Navigation. At this time, nine carriers by water were listed in *Slater's Directory*. They operated vessels along the inland waterways to such places as Shrewsbury, Gloucester, Worcester, Hereford, London, Bath, Bradford-on-Avon, Hungerford, Newbury, Reading, Chippenham, Swindon and Calne. Twenty-five years later, railway carriers had taken over much of the inland waterways carrying trade as there were only four carriers by water listed for Bristol in the *Post Office Directory of Somersetshire and Bristol* of 1875 compared with 21 railway carriers at Bristol.

An increased volume of trade and an increase in the size of steamships led to improvements in the City Docks. Under the superintendence of the Docks engineer, Thomas Howard, new works were carried out at Cumberland Basin and a new entrance lock was opened, from the river to the basin, on 19 July 1873. The

16 This view of the church of St Nicholas dates from the early 1900s. Craft in front of the church and along Welsh Back, on the left, include narrowboats, sailing vessels and barges.

construction of deep-water wharves followed, which were able to accommodate large vessels. By the end of the 19th century, the waterfront at Bristol was certainly different from what it had been a hundred years earlier. For instance, a visitor to the City Docks, at the end of the Edwardian era, would have been very much aware of the importance of the grain trade. A noteworthy building along the waterside, built on the site of the old Wapping dock, was the Corporation Granary, a huge red-brick building over 200ft long and nearly 100ft wide, which could store 15,000 tons of wheat. This granary had elevating machinery and electrically driven belts for sending the grain to different parts of the premises. Some of the imported grain never went into storage, but was loaded right away into railway trucks for onward conveyance.

Over the centuries, besides being a leading port, Bristol was also important for shipbuilding. William Matthews' *New History of Bristol* gave details of the city's dockyards at the end of the 18th century:

> On the banks of both Rivers are several Dock-yards, and dry and floating Docks for building and repairing the Ships. There are two or three by the Froom, besides the various Docks at Wapping by the Avon, where is also a spacious wet Dock with double gates lately built to keep Ships constantly afloat. Below these beyond Limekiln-Dock towards the Hotwells, is a large floating Dock, that will contain 40 sail of stout Ships deeply laden, and which in Jan. 1769 received a 64 gun Ship with ease through its gates. Here are also other Docks, a dry Dock that will hold a 74 gun Ship; and Dock yards where have been built several Ships of War for Government. At all these places, Ship-building and repairing are carried on with great spirit, skill and industry.

Among the shipbuilders of 1794, listed in William Matthews' *New History of Bristol*, was James Martin Hilhouse who operated Hotwells Dockyard between 1772 and 1823. By 1810, the firm of Hilhouse & Sons had three dockyards including the Limekiln dock. In 1820, the company developed a new site opposite Hotwells and their original dockyard and their Wapping premises were relinquished. Charles Hill took over the business in the mid-19th century and the New Dockyard became the Albion Dockyard. Other 19th-century shipbuilding sites, by the Floating Harbour, included Mardyke, Sea Banks, Marble Yard, Canon's Marsh, Teast's Docks, Tomb's Dock, Wapping Shipyard, Cumberland Yard, Wapping Dock, Wapping, Great Western Yard, Bedminster Yard, Vauxhall Yard, Nova Scotia and Cumberland Iron-Works.

The first steamer, built specifically to cross the Atlantic to New York, was built in Bristol. The *Great Western*, a wooden paddle steamer designed by Isambard Kingdom Brunel, was launched from William Patterson's yard at Wapping on 19 July 1837. Designed by Brunel and built as a companion to the *Great Western*, the much larger *Great Britain* was floated out of her dock on 19 July 1843 in the presence of Prince Albert, the Prince Consort. The four-decked steamship was the largest in the world at that time. She was also the first screw-propelled wrought iron ship to be built for ocean travel, having 252 berths for passengers and 130 for crew. On the second deck were two promenade saloons – the aft saloon was for first-class passengers, while the forward saloon was for those travelling second-class.

17 According to *Chilcott's Descriptive History of Bristol*, the four-masted *Great Western* was 236ft in length and 59ft in breadth over the paddle boxes. She had engines and machinery of 450 horse power, while each of the four boilers held 20 tons of water and weighed 24 tons. There was room for 800 tons of coal, stowed in iron boxes, which was sufficient for 25 days' consumption. Despite the amount of space devoted to the latter, the *Great Western* had 136 passenger berths as well as cabins for officers and crew. The saloon was 63ft in length by 32ft in breadth and was 'most splendidly fitted up in the style of the age of Louis Quatorze'.

The third deck held the Grand Saloon and the Forward Saloon for dining, while the fourth deck was for cargo of which the *Great Britain* could carry 1,200 tons besides coal weighing 1,000 tons. When the *Great Britain* was about to leave Bristol in 1844, it was found that she was so large that she couldn't get out of the lock. Masonry had to be taken from the lock walls before she could pass through to the tidal section of the river.

For some years, the *Great Britain* was used in the trans-Atlantic passenger trade. Between 1852 and 1876 she was used to carry emigrants to Australia and was also chartered as a troopship from 1854-5 during the Crimean War. However, after 1886, the once-prestigious *Great Britain* lay at the Falkland Islands and was used to store coal and wool. In 1970, she was towed 7,500 miles back to Bristol and brought into the Great Western Dock on 19 July of that year, 127 years to the day of her launch. During the intervening years, the *Great Britain* has undergone much restoration and is a celebrated attraction in the City Docks today.

According to Grahame Farr, in *Bristol Shipbuilding in the Nineteenth Century* (1971), 279 vessels are known to have been built at Bristol between 1839 and 1860. Two hundred and twelve of this number were built of wood and 64 were made of iron, while one steam vessel had a composite construction. The composition of the remaining two ships is unknown. The number of craft being built in Bristol dropped in the period between 1860 and 1899. Then, Grahame Farr noted, there were about 114 steam vessels and 119 sailing or 'dumb' vessels constructed in the Bristol shipbuilding industry. Shipbuilders during the latter half of the 19th century included Charles Hill & Son at the Albion Dockyard and the Limekiln Dockyard, George A. Miller & Co. at Dean's Marsh dry dock, William Patterson at the Great

Western Dockyard, John Payne at Vauxhall Yard, Coronation Road, G.K. Stothert & Co. at Hotwells and Wapping Dock Co. at Wapping.

Both before and after the construction of the Floating Harbour, ferries were used to cross stretches of water in Bristol. The ancient ferry from Queen Street to Temple Back appears to have been a crossing to Counterslip, which was formerly 'Countess-slip'. When St Philip's Bridge was opened, in 1841, this ferry was no longer needed. In 1717, a slip was made for the ferry operating between the Welsh Back and Redcliff Back, while another was made on the Grove for the ferry, which was known as the Guinea Street Ferry. Both these ferries were still in use in the early 20th century. The Gibb Ferry, at the end of Prince Street, was owned by the Dean and Chapter of Bristol Cathedral. When the Floating Harbour was created, the Dock Company erected a wooden bridge at this crossing and the Cathedral authorities took the tolls from pedestrians, while the Company received the tolls from vehicles. Eventually, a toll-free swing bridge, opened in 1879, replaced the wooden structure.

18   Clifton Suspension Bridge and Rownham Ferry, c.1912. Rownham Ferry was repositioned in 1873 when there were alterations to the entrance to Cumberland Basin. At low tide, the ferry became a bridge of boats, while at high tide the passage could be dangerous because of the current. The River Avon is a tributary of the River Severn, which has the second greatest tidal rise and fall of any river in the world. There is a tidal range of about 50ft at the Severn Estuary at spring tides, while on these occasions the range is about 40ft on the River Avon.

Rownham Ferry, in existence for centuries, was sometimes used as a horse ferry as it was originally in a spot where horsemen were tempted to ford the river, at low water, rather than make a long detour to Bristol Bridge. In the mid-19th century, people would cross the river by Rownham Ferry to visit the strawberry gardens at Ashton where strawberry and cream teas could be enjoyed. The ferry at Rownham was moved a little upstream in 1873. In Edwardian times, despite a considerable amount of its former passengers using the newly opened Ashton Swing Bridge, the ferry continued to be frequented by travellers using the Clifton Bridge railway station. It stopped plying for trade on 31 December 1932.

By the first decade of the 20th century, there were other ferries in existence. One carried passengers from Broad Quay to the Butts, while others went from Prince's Wharf to Canon's Marsh and from Canon's Marsh, by the Gas works, to Wapping. Another ferry crossed the water from Mardyke to the Cumberland Road side of the Floating Harbour. At this time, there was also a ferry across the New Cut from Cumberland Road to St Paul's Church, Coronation Road, which was known as Coronation Ferry.

Today, ferry boats are still part of the city's waterside scene. They are a good way of moving between the attractions around Bristol's Floating Harbour, which include the SS *Great Britain* and Maritime Heritage Centre, the *Matthew*, a replica of John Cabot's sailing ship, The Industrial Museum, the British Empire and Commonwealth Museum and the Watershed Media Centre plus St Mary Redcliffe Church and Bristol Cathedral.

The Bristol Avon's most famous bridge, Clifton Suspension Bridge, is downriver from the Floating Harbour. Designed by Isambard Kingdom Brunel, the foundation stone of the buttress, on the Somerset side of the river, was laid in 1836, but the project was abandoned in 1853. The Clifton Suspension Bridge Company was formed in 1860 and over the next four years the structure was eventually finished. It was opened with much rejoicing on 8 December 1864 and has been a great attraction ever since. Unfortunately, it has also proved to be a fatal attraction for those intent on committing suicide by jumping from the bridge. However, not all who attempted this perished. In 1885, a young woman was saved when her dress acted as a parachute when she dropped from the bridge. Two sisters who were thrown over the bridge, by their father, also survived as they were picked up by a pilot who was passing below the bridge.

Clifton Suspension Bridge looks over the area along the River Avon known as Hotwells. In the past, this location was renowned for the medicinal spring, at the bottom of St Vincent's Rock, which gave the place its name. In 1695, the Merchant Venturers of Bristol, lords of the manor of Clifton, granted a building lease to some Bristol citizens who erected the Hotwell House, which had pumps to raise the water. The 18th-century author, Daniel Defoe, wrote: 'Not many years since, this Spring lay open at the Foot of the Rock and was covered by the salt water at every tide.' He added, 'The Well is secur'd, and a good Pump is fix'd in it, so that they have the Water pure and unmix'd from the Spring itself, and they export vast Quantities;

for this Water keeps its Virtue better than that of *Bath*.' The author remarked that a vast number of Bristol-made glass bottles were used 'for sending the Water of St *Vincent's* Rock, not only all over *England*, but we may say, all over the World'.

In 1789, William Barrett, in *The History and Antiquities of the City of Bristol*, observed: 'It is on the north side, at the bottom of the rock within the channel of the Avon on its bank, the Hotwell spring rises up with some force from beneath, upwards of ten feet above low water and about twenty-six feet below high water.' The author commented on 'the celebrated uses of Bristol Hotwell Water'. He noted that it could be used 'to temper an hot acrimonious blood, restrain haemorrhages and seminal weaknesses, to cure the hectic fever and sweats, relieve consumptive people if the disease be inveterate, cure them if recent'. William Barrett also stated that 'above all its virtue in the diabetes has been deemed unquestionable'.

The author of *The History and Antiquities of the City of Bristol* commented further on the situation at Hotwells:

> Patients with these complaints in the summer months flock hither from every part of the kingdom, where and at Clifton, a healthy and delightful situation, most elegant lodging-houses and every convenient accommodation for families that arrive can be had at the shortest notice; the pleasant rides on the neighbouring downs, the amusements, the music at the Long Rooms, the balls, assemblies etc. make it also the resort of pleasure as well as the retreat of the sick and valetudinary.

However, in 1790 a new tenant, Samuel Powell, took over the spa at Hotwells and the charges for drinking the mineral water were greatly increased. This led to a decline in the visitors attracted to the location. John Latimer, in *The Annals of Bristol in the Eighteenth Century*, remarked: 'Many upper-class families that had flocked to the pump-room in the search of pleasure rather than of health declined to pay the enhanced charge, and betook themselves to other watering places, and their example became contagious.'

After the old Hotwell House was demolished in 1822, there was an attempt to bring back interest in the spa. In 1844, *Chilcott's Descriptive History of Bristol* noted:

> The new Hotwell House is situated immediately behind the site of the old Well House; it is built in the Tuscan order, and presents a handsome front of Bath stone. The ground floor contains a very good Pump Room, and well-arranged hot and cold baths; the upper portion of the house is appropriated to domestic purposes, and is let furnished, being peculiarly suitable to invalids, whose object is to give the waters a fair trial.

These new premises survived less than half a century, being demolished in 1867 in order for Hotwell Point to be removed to render navigation along the river safer. Later in the century, the water from the hot spring was tapped by boring through the rock to a great depth. It was pumped up to the Clifton Grand Spa Pump Room, which was opened in 1894 near the upper station of the new Clifton Rocks Railway, a funicular railway running between Hotwells and Sion Hill. Both the railway and the spa were promoted by publisher, George Newnes, M.P. for Newmarket. The striking pump room of the Clifton Grand Spa and Hydro was built in the Corinthian style of architecture, its roof being supported by 20 massive marble columns with decorated capitals. Here, the Hotwell mineral water could be obtained from a marble fountain set in an ornamental alcove.

Since the establishment of the steam packets, in the first half of the 19th century, Hotwells had been enlivened by the arrival of visitors. At high water, the banks of the river and the landing places were crowded with folk either greeting or bidding farewell to friends and relations. There were a number of hotels in the vicinity in the mid-19th century, including the *Royal Gloucester Hotel*, Rownham Place, the *Cumberland Hotel*, Cumberland Basin, the *Steam Packet Hotel*, Hotwell Road and the *York Hotel*, Dowry Square.

One of the travellers who took a steam packet from Bristol was Louisa Anne Twamley who wrote *An Autumn Ramble by the Wye* (1839). In this book, the authoress commented:

> Our Bristol packet, though far from first-rate, was spacious and carried some very tolerable musicians. We quickly passed down the Avon, gazing at old Bristol, new Clifton, and its yet newer Suspension Bridge, or rather the commencement of that grand undertaking; for at that time only one single cord or chain, had been flung across the river, at an airy height above us ... Those cliffs and precipices of the Avon, are grandly beautiful, and amply reward a tourist, even for a long circuit made to pass them; and the windings of the river, incessantly offer new phases of their majestic beauty, till we emerge into the wide estuary of the Severn, to which the Avon brings its tributary waters.

Charles Frederick Cliffe, the author of *The Book of South Wales, the Bristol Channel, Monmouthshire, and the Wye* travelled along the Avon, too. In 1847, he wrote about his journey downriver in a chapter entitled 'Voyage down the Avon'.

> We are now afloat. The rope is cast off – we move on 'at all speed' – the crowded pier-heads disappear ... In two or three hours this fine tidal river, now brim-full, will sink almost to a rivulet, with immense muddy banks. Despite this drawback – to which the Wye is also liable below Tintern – the scenery does not suffer very seriously. The 'grand scene' is at Saint Vincent's Rocks, which are impressive even under the flattest light ... Before we depart we must, in common with every admirer of the beautiful rocky valley we have been passing through, lift our voices against the cupidity which has remorselessly disfigured it with enormous quarries, chiefly for the supply of turnpike roads. Even Saint Vincent's Rocks have been threatened within the last few years: and the massive bluff, which was to carry the Suspension Bridge, was labelled 'good road stone at 9d. per ton!'

In late Victorian times, steamers left the port of Bristol for a variety of places, which included Belfast, Dublin, Glasgow, Liverpool, Montreal and New York. There were regular services to these destinations, in Edwardian times, when steamers also went to Hamburg, West Indies, Central America, South America, South Africa, Australia and New Zealand. In 1906, for instance, there were fortnightly passenger trips between Bristol (Avonmouth Dock) and Kingston, Jamaica, calling at Turks Island, on the outward journey, and every six weeks at Bermuda. Other fortnightly trips, from Avonmouth, by steamers carrying goods, were to Montreal in summer and Portland, Maine in winter. The same year, steamers left the port of Bristol for Buenos Ares and Montevideo, monthly, while the Bristol City Line steamers went to New York weekly.

During the summer months, trips by paddle steamer to places of interest along the Bristol Channel could be taken from Bristol. In the early 20th century, P. & A. Campbell Ltd were the main operators of these Bristol Channel excursions. Places visited by the paddle steamers included Clevedon, Weston-super-Mare, Minehead, Lynmouth, Ilfracombe, Clovelly, Tenby, the Mumbles, Newport, Cardiff and Chepstow. A daily service between Bristol, Weston-super-Mare and Cardiff was maintained during the season. Old postcards of the time often show the paddle steamers with a view of Clifton Suspension Bridge in the background.

Looking downstream from Clifton Suspension Bridge, Leigh Woods are on the left bank of the Avon Gorge. Just past the bridge, on the same bank as the woods, is Nightingale Valley. In Victorian times, those who enjoyed walking could cross the river by Rownham Ferry, turn to the right and walk between the river and the woods to the little cottages on its edge. After perhaps taking a cup of tea here, visitors would walk up the combe near the cottages. This beauty spot

19   This engraving of the Avon Gorge and Nightingale Valley, a beauty spot in Leigh Woods, was included in *A Brief Historical Sketch of Bristol with the New Picture of Clifton, and Stranger's Guide* by John Morgan. The Observatory can be seen on the left of the view. Nightingale Valley was a routeway in ancient times as it led to a ford on the river at low water, which was a communication between the three forts on the heights above, Burgh Walls and Stokeleigh Camp, on the Somerset bank, and Clifton Camp on the Gloucestershire side of the River Avon.

was a favourite venue for picnic parties on summer evenings. Known by some as Happy Valley and by others as Nightingale Valley, it was said that the reverberation produced by the beautiful notes of the nightingale, in this location, produced a delightful effect.

On the Clifton side of the river is the Observatory, which was known as West's Observatory in Victorian times. Containing a variety of optical instruments, including telescopes and a camera obscura, it became a favourite venue for generations of Bristolians and visitors to Clifton. In the mid-1830s, William West, the proprietor, had a passage excavated from the Observatory to a previously inaccessible cave on the face of the cliff below, overlooking the Avon Gorge. The cave was known by various names such as Ghyston's Cave, Giant's Cave or Fox Hole. An iron railing across the opening in the cliff protected visitors from falling down the precipice. In Edwardian times, the admission to the Observatory was sixpence, while it cost a further sixpence to go along the subterranean passage leading to the cave.

Visitors to Clifton Downs would look out for Cook's Folly, downriver from the Observatory. This 17th-century tower, built on a height, had a curious legend attached to it. It was said that a man called Cook had dreamed that he would die from the bite of a viper so he erected the tower and shut himself up in it. He received his food, fuel and other necessities by letting down a basket. However, despite these precautions, the day came when a viper, hidden in some faggots of wood, sprang out and the fatal wound was inflicted on the recluse. In another version of the tale, Cook was told that his unborn son would not live to see his 21st birthday and that a 'silent secret foe' would strike him dead in his 20th year. To avoid the fulfilment of the prediction, the boy was immured in the tower, during that year, only to perish, on the day before his 21st birthday, by being struck by a viper hidden in a basket of fuel. There would appear to be no truth in either story, but the tale encouraged visitors to the spot. In the mid-19th century, admittance to the tower cost 3d. From this height, the uninterrupted and expansive view of King Road, the safe anchorage for ships at the mouth of the Avon, could be seen and this was enhanced when vessels were in full sail. Those who climbed the tower could also enjoy the sight of the Welsh mountains on the other side of the Severn.

A little further downstream, at Sea Mills, the River Trym joins the River Avon on its right bank. A Roman station called Abona is thought to have been situated alongside this little river. In 1712, a large floating dock was started here. According to William Barrett, in *The History and Antiquities of the City of Bristol*, the dock was 'capable of containing several score sail afloat'. The author remarked that ships were admitted 'with tide into the dock ... through very large gates; which being shut down they ride safe moored, and by the help of cranes they were unloaden there into large lighters or boats of burden, and by them the goods and wares were brought up to the merchants store-houses.' William Barrett noted that the floating dock was little used in 1788. It was subsequently abandoned.

20   At the end of the Sea Mills reach, the River Avon curves around the Horseshoe Bend. As ships became larger, they found difficulty in getting around the bend. Near the end of the bend, on the right-hand bank, the whitewashed Powder House can be seen. This was where ships coming into Bristol once left their explosives and received them again on their outward voyage.

A short distance downriver of Sea Mills, the Avon makes a spectacular horseshoe bend past Shirehampton Park and into the stretch of the river called Hung Road. At the time of the French and Spanish wars of the early 17th century, the Bristol privateers moored in Hung Road, while the West Indiamen used to tranship their cargoes here in the days when large vessels couldn't sail up to the city. Long after the Floating Harbour was constructed, the massive iron rings, on the bank of the river at Hung Road, bore witness to the use of this reach of the Avon as an anchorage.

Shirehampton, on the same bank as Sea Mills, is set back from the river, but its centuries-old inn, the *Lamplighters*, is on the riverside. The unusual name of the inn is said to derive from an 18th-century Bristol tinman, Joseph Swetnam, who had made a profit from lighting oil lamps in several Bristol parishes. The money was spent on building a house in the country, which was known as *Lamplighter's Hall*. Over the years, the premises were much frequented by pleasure parties from Bristol and by societies, which held annual dinners there. The ferry, between Shirehampton and Pill, which used to cross the Avon from this inn, closed in 1974.

21   This view shows pilot skiffs in Pill Harbour. *J. Wright & Co.'s Bristol Directory 1901* listed 22 licensed pilots for the Port of Bristol and the Bristol Channel along with the names and numbers of their skiffs. Among these Pill pilots were those with the local surnames Carey, Thayer, Dickens, Craddy, Bailey and Rowles. The latter surname also belonged to boat builders in Pill whose premises can be seen in the background on the left of this view.

As the Avon nears its mouth, the land alongside the river is indented by 'pills'. These are tidal creeks along the bank of the river. Just after the Horseshoe Bend is Chapel Pill on the Somerset side of the river. The name of this small creek is derived from the 13th-century St Katherine's Chapel, built for the use of mariners and now long gone. The full name of Pill, opposite Shirehampton, is Crockerne Pill. Grahame Farr, in *Somerset Harbours* (1954), observed that one view of the origin of the name was that it came from 'Krokr', a Norse name meaning 'big strong man'. The men of Pill certainly had to have been fit and strong for their occupations as pilots in the Bristol Channel.

In 1791, in *The History and Antiquities of the County of Somerset*, the Rev. John Collinson noted:

> Upon the river Avon ... stands the hamlet of CROCKERNE-PILL, the buildings of which chiefly arose in the last century for the habitation of mariners, whose business consists in piloting vessels to and from Bristol, and down the Channel, sometimes as low as the island of Lundy, in which a great number of towing boats and yawls are constantly employed, besides skiffs which ply down the channel; in speculation for the arrival of vessels.

Generations of Pill families had menfolk who were pilots. Their dangerous occupation took them not only out into the Bristol Channel but beyond that, too. On occasion they sailed as far as Liverpool and the south coast of Ireland. They also were known to range beyond Land's End and into the English Channel. The pilot skiffs were manned by two westernmen or one westernman and a boy who would bring the vessel back after the pilot had been landed on board a ship. Westernmen was the name given to the men who assisted the pilot. Those who manned the Pill boats must have been hardy and courageous, braving the Bristol Channel in all weathers.

The preacher, John Wesley, however, had a different opinion of the inhabitants of Pill. In 1755, he remarked: 'I rode over to Pill, a place famous from generation to generation, even as Kingswood itself, for stupid, brutal, abandoned wickedness.' Another visitor to Pill was newspaper editor, Joseph Leech, who was the author of *The Churchgoer. Rural Rides; or Calls at Country Churches*, published in 1847. He called at Pill, in 1845, and commented on the traces of filth, vice and intemperance, which could be seen there. However, this author might have been biased, having been pelted with potato skins by local children during his visit! Pill men, though, certainly had a reputation for rough behaviour. In 1836, when the first steam tug was introduced for towing ships, they boarded the vessel and cut her adrift. Prior to the introduction of steam towing, ships were pulled along the River Avon, between Bristol and the river mouth, by Pill men in small rowing boats, or by 'hobblers' on the river bank, towing with ropes.

Ernest Walls, in *The Bristol Avon*, referred to a 'desolate and wind-swept level' broken by 'mud-banked pills' on the Somerset side of the river as the Avon approached its confluence with the Severn. Nearing the end of his short 'Voyage down the Avon', Charles Frederick Cliffe wrote about the last reach of the Avon 'which here widens greatly, and has always a picturesque character when the tide is up, although the river banks have become low and tame – the "sea-walls" of marsh land'. He added that there were two entrances to King Road, 'the noble roadstead outside'. He noted that the southernmost entrance, 'the Swash', could only be traversed by shipping at certain states of the tide, when there was deep water over it, and that, as a saving of about a mile was effected by taking this course, the steamers always pursued it when they could.

In the mid-19th century, when Charles Frederick Cliffe wrote his account, there was a small island at the mouth of the River Avon called Dunball. Until around 1760, this had been part of the southern mainland, but it had been gradually cut off from the Somerset bank when the river started to make a new course. It was this channel that became known as the Swash. Around 1867, the original mouth of the Avon between Dunball and the Gloucestershire bank started to silt up very quickly with the result that the Swash became the only channel out to the River Severn and Dunball became part of the northern mainland.

Since this time, there has been much change in the area around the mouth of the Avon. These changes include the building of a bridge to take the M5 across the river and the construction of docks at Avonmouth and at Portbury. In the late 19th century, the provision of new docks was necessary as ships were increasing in size and better facilities were needed than the City Docks in Bristol could provide. The construction of Avonmouth's first dock began in 1868. It took nine years to build, during which time there were setbacks when one of the quay walls sank and bulged outwards, while another collapsed. The area of the dock was 16 acres and its lock measured 454ft by 70ft. On 24 February 1877, crowds gathered to watch the paddle steamer, *Juno*, leave Cumberland Basin carrying the Mayor of Bristol and his 450 guests to the opening ceremony of the new Avonmouth Dock. At Avonmouth, another multitude assembled. It was the beginning of a new era of prosperity for the Port of Bristol. Two years later, a new dock was opened at Portishead.

Steamships continued to increase in size so, between 1902 and 1908, Avonmouth Docks were expanded. The Royal Edward Dock was opened on 9 July 1908 by King Edward VII, accompanied by Queen Alexandra, during a three-day visit to Avonmouth and Bristol. This new dock covered almost twice the area of the original dock and its entrance lock measured 875ft by 100ft. During the second half of the 20th century, however, with the increase in size of container vessels, a new dock was, once again, required. This was constructed, over a period of five years, on the opposite side of the river from Avonmouth. On 8 August 1977, in her Silver Jubilee Year, Queen Elizabeth II, escorted by Prince Philip, opened the Royal Portbury Dock. This deep-water dock can accommodate huge ships and its lock, measuring 1,200ft long and 140ft wide, is the largest lock in Great Britain.

22 On the occasion of the opening of the Royal Edward Dock at Avonmouth in 1908, King Edward VII and Queen Alexandra stayed aboard the Royal Yacht, *Victoria & Albert*, which was moored in the entrance lock to the new dock.

23   The Severn and the Avon from Durdham Down, Clifton. Cook's Folly can be seen on the right.

Having reached the end of my historical journey along the Bristol Avon, my thoughts turn to those whose journeys were just beginning when they reached the mouth of the river. In particular I think of my ancestors, those courageous Pill pilots who daily braved the perils of the Bristol Channel and beyond. My thoughts touch on my 19th-century Somerset forebears who crossed the River Severn to seek work in the Welsh coal mines and on those who emigrated from the West Country to North America in search of a better life. Perhaps the following scene, described by Louisa Anne Twamley in *An Autumn Ramble along the River Wye*, met their eyes:

> Vessels on their way to Bristol entering the river, and those being towed out, the larger by steamers, the smaller by row-boats, add great animation to the scene. The waters of the Bristol channel spread to the southern horizon, specked with white-gleaming sails; and the Denny rock lifts its dark head above the waves midway between the Gloucester and Monmouth shores.

SHERSTON MAGNA

24 The embattled central tower of Sherston Church looks over High Street in this view dating from c.1909. On the extreme right is the *Forester's Arms*, which has a striking late 17th-century shell hood over its doorway. Further along this side of the wide High Street, the village school is conspicuous with its tall windows and twin bell towers. In 1903, the mixed elementary school could hold 270 children. The schoolmaster at this time was George Dear, while the infants' mistress was Miss E.M. Morris.

25 This view of Noble Street, from the church tower, dates from c.1920. It looks in a south-easterly direction towards the infant River Avon. A bridge at Tanners Hill, further down the slope, crosses the river. In the days before the bridge was built, there was a ford over the river. The road, on the left of the picture, is Bustlers Hill, leading to Chippenham, while Thompson's Hill, on the right, goes past Hill House Farm. Sherston's Primitive Methodist Chapel is among the buildings on the right.

26 The tall spire of the church of St Mary the Virgin at Tetbury is a landmark in the surrounding countryside. Rising to 186ft, the spire is said to be the fourth highest in the country. Seven of the bells in the tower date from 1722, while the eighth dates from 1803.

27 A focal point of Tetbury is the 17th-century Market House, which stands on stone pillars. Markets for wool and yarn were once held here, while the affairs of the parish were transacted in its principal room. In his history of Tetbury, published in 1857, the Rev. Alfred T. Lee commented, 'It is much to be wished that the Church and Town clocks kept the same time, but at present they are at perpetual variance.' This old postcard view of the distinctive building dates from c.1913.

28 Visitors to Tetbury in the early 20th century sent their friends and relatives postcards of this popular view of Chipping Steps bordered by 17th-century houses. The Chipping Steps lead up to the north-east corner of The Chipping. The latter's name is derived from the Saxon for market. In the past, it was the site of cattle markets and annual fairs. *Pigot & Co.'s Directory* of 1844 noted that fairs were held on Ash Wednesday and 22 July and that statute meetings for hiring servants were held 'on the Wednesday next before the 5th April, and on the Wednesdays before and after Old Michaelmas Day'. By 1885, there was only the Ash Wednesday fair and the hiring fairs, known as Mop Fairs, were held on the Wednesdays before and after 11 October. Mop fairs are still held in Tetbury, but now they are fun fairs.

29 An early 20th-century view of Silver Street showing the Green in the foreground. The building with twin gables, in the far distance, is the *Crown* on Gumstool Hill. Silver Street had a number of tradespeople in 1906. These included Albert Chapman, trap proprietor, Frederick William Cull, fried fish dealer, and Thomas Topps, greengrocer, while Edward Webb ran the *Talbot*, a commercial hotel.

30 Fox Hill, leading out of Tetbury, takes the traveller in the direction of Malmesbury. The road crosses the stripling Avon by the Wiltshire Bridge where the letters G and W, on the north parapet of the bridge, are a reminder that this was once the boundary between Gloucestershire and Wiltshire.

MALMESBURY

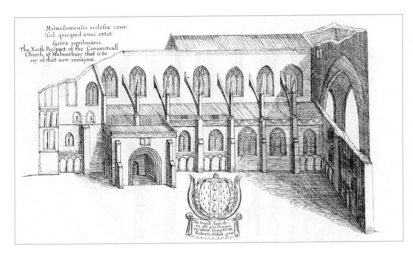

31 This old print of the north prospect of Malmesbury Abbey is from *Monasticon Anglicanum or the History of the Ancient Abbies, Monasteries, Hospital, Cathedral and Collegiate Churches with their Dependencies in England and Wales*, which was published in 1718. Dissolved in 1539, the abbey and its surrounding lands and buildings were sold to William Stumpe. This wealthy clothier gave the nave of the abbey to the town to be its parish church as the original 13th-century parish church of St Paul was in a state of decay.

32 Malmesbury Cross, erected in the late 15th century, is octagonal in shape. It is of special architectural interest as it is one of only three similar crosses in England. John Leland, the 16th-century writer, observed that it was a 'costley peace of worke' and for poor folks 'to stande dry when rayne cummith'. This print was engraved by James Newton and published by S. Hooper of 212 High Holborn, London on 5 September 1785.

33　The *King's Arms*, an old coaching inn, is on the left of this view, which looks up High Street towards Malmesbury Cross and the abbey. In 1903, the inn was advertised as a 'family & commercial hotel & posting house', with good stabling. Its famous hotelier was listed as Henry Jones, in *Kelly's Directory of Wiltshire* for that year, but he was widely known as Harry. On the opposite side of High Street, towards the Cross, is the *George Hotel*, another coaching inn. It was kept by George William Bishop, in 1903. By 1920, George Furber was running this establishment.

34　Harry Jones, the proprietor of the *King's Arms Hotel*, standing outside his premises. Dr Bernulf Hodge in *A History of Malmesbury* noted that the hotelier always wore a white 'beaver hat' with bottle-green coat and breeches. This old postcard was posted in 1912.

35   Malmesbury from Daniel's Well, *c*.1905. The Sherston branch of the infant River Avon is in the foreground of this view. The name of Daniel's Well is said to derive from Daniel, an early abbot of Malmesbury, who used to immerse himself in a spring in this locality and spend the night there, even in the winter time.

CHIPPENHAM

36   This view of Back Avon Bridge, with River Street in the background, dates from *c*.1906. However, this peaceful scene at the footbridge must have been very different in times of flood.

37 The stone-built Town Bridge, over the Avon at Chippenham, was widened at the end of the 18th century. Additions at this time included a parapet wall, stone balustrade and more arches. According to Arnold Platts, in *A History of Chippenham A.D. 853-1946*, oil lamps lit the bridge in 1799 and gas lamps were used by 1834. The tall building on the left, formerly the Bridge Cloth Factory, once housed Chippenham's condensed milk factory.

38 The factory, operated by the Anglo-Swiss Condensed Milk Company at Bath Road, was the first in England to manufacture condensed milk. In 1905, this business merged with that of Henri Nestlé. During the early years of the 20th century, the milk was delivered to the premises by horse-drawn vehicles. Local author, Arnold Platts, observed that the line of milk carts would often extend to the Town Hall in one direction, to the railway viaduct in another direction and also along the Bath Road for a considerable distance.

39 Before the construction of Chippenham's new Town Hall, the mid-15th-century Yelde Hall, in the Market Place, had served the town in that capacity. On the window above the door are the Borough Arms. In 1891, this half-timbered gabled building became the headquarters of the Volunteer Rifle Corps. Recruitment posters can be seen on its walls. Arnold Platts, in *A History of Chippenham A.D. 853-1946*, noted that, in 1912, the fence in front of the building was taken down. This photograph, therefore, dates from before that year.

40 The opening of the great Cheese Market at Chippenham on 12 September 1850 was reported in the *Illustrated London News* on 21 September 1850:

Many persons anticipated, from the large supply of cheese at the previous market, that the present one would not show so great an increase. These anticipations, however, were not realised; for full 400 tons were brought in to this day's market, and the great bulk sold readily at the following quotations: – Broad doubles, 42s. to 51s.; prime Cheddar, 50s. to 57s.; ditto, thin, 36s. to 40s.; ditto, loaves, 50s. to 56s. per cwt. The town, as on the preceding day, presented a most animated appearance. The immense quantity of waggons, carts, gigs &c., which came pouring in, and the throng of business persons traversing the streets – which remained gaily decorated, as on the preceding day, with brilliant banners – rendered the scene strikingly beautiful and picturesque.

41 In early Edwardian times, there was a market at Chippenham on the second Friday each month for cheese and cattle, while a market was held on the last Friday in every month for cattle alone. An annual cattle show was held during the last week in November. This photograph of market day at Chippenham dates from *c.*1904.

42 The *Bear* and the *Angel* were once coaching inns on the road to London. In 1901, Henry Bailey was hotel keeper at the *Bear*, the three-gabled building at 12 Market Place on the left of this view. He advertised good stabling and traps for hire. Richard Careless was hotel proprietor at the *Angel Hotel*, the striking porticoed building, on the right, at 8 Market Place. Here, visitors were assured that a 'bus met all trains.

43 Isambard Kingdom Brunel's railway viaduct can be seen in the background of this early 20th-century view of New Road. On the right, near the viaduct, are the premises of W.J. Ball & Son. In 1903, W.J. Ball was a milliner, draper and house furnisher in New Road. Apart from two horse-drawn vehicles and a lady with a bicycle, traffic in this shop-lined street is noticeably absent.

LACOCK

44 The east front of Lacock Abbey from the River Avon, c.1920s. The abbey was built on a meadow bearing the delightful name of Snaylesmeade.

45 High Street, *c*.1904. The tall building, on the right of this view, is the *Red Lion*. Its striking red-brick frontage was built in the 18th century, covering a building constructed in earlier times. Coaches used to stop at the inn when Lacock was on the road between London and Bath. After a new road to Bath was made, in the late 18th century, the old route fell into disuse. In 1903, Mrs Ruth Rowlett was proprietress of the inn, while John Butler was at the *Coffee Tavern* next door.

46 Lacock's Market Cross, which once stood outside the *Red Lion*, was restored in the late 19th century. This view of children, seated around its stepped base, dates from *c*.1904. The Market Cross can now be found in the playground of the village school, which is set back from High Street.

47   The *George Inn*, in West Street, dates from the 14th century. This view of the ancient hostelry, the oldest in the village, dates from the first decade of the 20th century when the licensee was the aptly named Albert Beer. A feature of the inn is an open fireplace with a tread wheel. In times past, a little dog ran around the wheel to turn the spit where meat was cooking.

48   The Old Market House, built in the 14th century, is on the right of this view of East Street. Formerly a tithe barn, it was later used as a market hall and also for grain storage. The half-timbered Chamberlain's House, on the left, may have been the dwelling place of one of the officials of Lacock Abbey. This village street scene dates from *c.*1908.

49 Church Street, *c*.1904. A 14th-century cruck house is in the background of the picture. Constructed of wood, brick and stone, it displays an exposed cruck timber and is among the earliest dwellings in the village. The 15th-century gabled building, in the foreground of this view, is an historic timber-framed inn known today as *At the Sign of the Angel*. The inn, like some other buildings in Lacock, has a horse passage through the premises, which formerly gave access to stabling behind the property.

50 This view of Church Street, dating from *c*.1908, looks eastwards to St Cyriac's Church. The church was mainly constructed in the 15th century, the embattled tower being a 16th-century addition. The house with the dormer windows, next to the church, is said to be the oldest house in the village. Known as King John's Hunting Lodge, the main part of the building is of 13th-century construction, while the back of the building is a Tudor addition. In July 1996, Church Street was used for filming Jane Austen's *Emma*. Lacock has also been used for the filming of other period dramas such as *Pride and Prejudice* and *Moll Flanders*.

MELKSHAM

51 Melksham railway station, situated on the other side of the River Avon from the town, was on the Wilts, Somerset and Weymouth branch of the Great Western Railway. In 1903, the station master was Edwin Charles Beard.

52 A four-arched stone bridge with balustrades crosses the Avon at Melksham. The bridge was built around 1809 and widened in 1929. This view of the Town Bridge dates from c.1916.

53 In the early years of the 20th century, omnibuses to and from the *King's Arms* met the arrival and departure of the trains at Melksham railway station. One such omnibus can be seen in this view of High Street, which dates from *c*.1902. The *King's Arms*, in the Market Place, was described at this time as a 'family & commercial hotel & posting house'.

54 Melksham Picture Hall is shown on the right of this view of High Street. A large board outside advertises a film about Dick Turpin. In 1920, W.B. Dennis was manager of this establishment. Next door are the premises of the London Central Meat Company Ltd.

55   This view of the Market Place is dominated by the Town Hall. Erected in 1847 by a company of shareholders, the white freestone building cost £3,350 and was built to house a cheese market on the ground floor with a council chamber above. In 1920, the market was held on alternate Tuesdays in the month for cattle, sheep and pigs. A fair for cattle, sheep and horses was held in the Market Place on 27 July.

56   In early Edwardian times, the extensive iron foundry at Melksham gave employment to about 1,000 people. Spencer & Co. Limited were listed in *Kelly's Directory of Wiltshire* of 1903 as 'engineers & millwrights, manufacturers of steam engines, patent grain & warehousing machinery, hydraulic and other lifts & general machinery'. This old postcard view of men leaving the iron foundry was posted in 1915.

57 Rowing boats are moored against the bank in this Edwardian view of the River Avon at Staverton. A small section of the river is navigable here and still used for pleasure boating.

BRADFORD-ON-AVON

58 New Mills, 1893. In the latter half of the 19th century, New Mills, Abbey Mills and Church Street Mills were conducted by Ward & Taylor and, from 1888, by J.H. Willis. They had a reputation for producing substantial and elegantly finished cloth. The mills manufactured all kinds of fancy woollen trouserings, suitings, covert coatings and tweeds suitable for riding. They also turned out material for rough wear such as whipcords, buckskins, ribs, Bedford cords, saddle tweeds and stable suitings.

59 The nine-arched Town Bridge in the centre of Bradford-on-Avon is distinguished by the small domed building on its upriver side. This is sometimes called a chapel, but there is little evidence for its having a religious connection. It was the 17th-century writer, John Aubrey, who noted, perhaps incorrectly, that there was a 'little chapell' on the bridge. The Blind House, as it is known, has been used as a lock-up for unruly townsfolk and as a toll-house when animals were being taken to market.

60 Abbey Mill and Church Street Mills, 1893. These woollen mills were operated in conjunction with New Mills. Visitors to the mills would have seen the whole process of woollen cloth manufacture, from the first stage of scouring the wool when it arrived from Australia and the Cape, to the pressing and packing up of the cloth ready for it to be sent to the firm's customers in different parts of the world.

61 The Shambles has buildings dating from medieval times, but the half-timbered work above the shops, on the left, probably dates from the 17th century. In the 1930s, the tall Georgian building next to these shops was replaced by a new building housing the Post Office.

62 One of the most interesting features of Bradford-on-Avon is the tiny Saxon church of St Laurence, which is near the north-east end of the parish church. This early 20th-century view of the renowned Saxon church shows the roof mark of a cottage, which formerly adjoined the building. Noting its current use as a school, the Rev. W.H. Jones, in 1859, described the situation when the Saxon church was discovered:

> Hemmed in on every side by buildings of one kind or another, – on the south side by a sort of wing added to the original building (in which the schoolmaster's residence now is), and also by another building used as a coach-house; – on the north by a large shed, employed for the purposes of the neighbouring woollen factory; – the design and nature of the building escaped, till a very recent date, the notice of Archaeologists.

63 The 14th-century Tithe Barn once belonged to Barton Farm, a grange of Shaftesbury Abbey. Taxes, known as tithes, were paid to the Abbess of Shaftesbury in agricultural produce. The barn was also used for storing the crops yielded by the abbey's grange. Outside, the restored building is distinctive for the porches on both its north and south sides and for its roof tiled with local stone. Inside, the massive curved wooden beams of the ceiling are remarkable.

64 The proximity of the Kennet & Avon Canal, in the foreground, to the ancient Tithe Barn is shown here, while the River Avon can be seen to the left of the view. In the background is Newtown, which was developed in the 17th century when the town was enjoying a period of prosperity. Prominent in Newtown, in the early 20th century, were the premises of Wilkins Brothers & Hudson Ltd, brewers and maltsters, wine and spirit merchants and mineral water manufacturers.

65 Dating from the 14th century, the four-arched Barton Bridge was built to connect the grange and its tithe barn with the abbey's farm lands, which were situated to the north of the River Avon. In this view, dating from *c*.1916, the bridge carrying the line of the Great Western Railway can be seen beyond the old pack-horse bridge, while the boathouse of the Bradford Rowing Club is to the left of Barton Bridge.

66 Limpley Stoke once had a station on the Salisbury, Weymouth and Bath branch of the Great Western Railway, the line of which can be seen in this early 20th-century view of the Limply Stoke Valley. In the distance, on the right, is the Avon Mill also known as Limpley Stoke Mill. This former cloth mill was used as a saw mill and for the manufacture of rubber in the late 19th and early 20th centuries. The distinctive chimney stack no longer exists.

67 The West of England Hydropathic Establishment, which looked over the Avon valley, is featured on this old postcard view. The Hydro, as it was known, was established as a health resort in 1860. It had spacious grounds of 14 acres and there were facilities for tennis, boating and other outdoor amusements. Inside, a variety of baths could be taken and the services of experienced masseurs could be obtained. The message on the back of this old postcard reads: 'This is the Hydro where a lot of well to do people come for the winter. It is quite a healthy place. They don't take anyone there under £4 the week.'

68 In early Victorian times tolls had to be paid at the bridge, which crossed the Avon at Limpley Stoke. It cost one shilling for a waggon, coach or four-wheeled carriage to pass over and sixpence for a cart or two-wheeled vehicle. Horses could cross for a penny and foot passengers for a halfpenny. The toll for a score of sheep, lambs or pigs was five pence, while that for cattle was a halfpenny per beast. The stone-built three-arched bridge, shown here, replaced the former bridge. It was erected in 1858 and has been widened several times since then.

69   Dwellings, clinging to the sides of the valley, made the small village of Limpley Stoke look picturesque. The children in this early 20th-century view would probably have attended the village school, the mistress of which, in 1903, was Miss M.B. Clapp. At that time, mothers in the village would have done their shopping at the premises of John Wilkins, who was grocer and beer retailer, or at the Post Office run by William Henry Weston, stationer and newsagent. Fathers may have spent some time at the public house called the *Hop Pole*.

70   This old print of the Dundas Aqueduct, which carries the Kennet & Avon Canal over the River Avon, dates from *c*.1864. In the foreground, a narrowboat can be seen going under a small hump-backed bridge at the entrance to the Somersetshire Coal Canal, while a railway engine is steaming along in the lower right-hand corner of the picture.

71 The message on the back of this old postcard, sent to Bridgeport in the United States, reads, 'I went through this place last Sunday on the top of a trolley-car.' Bath was connected to surrounding villages by an electric tramway, which was opened in 1904, and there were many picturesque views along the different routes. The open-topped tram, in this view, is crossing Bathford Bridge over the By Brook. The latter was known in times past as the Box Brook. It rises, in two streams, south of Tormarton, and is joined by another stream, which rises south of Marshfield. In the background, on the ridge above Bathford, is Brown's Folly, built by local landowner, Wade Brown, in the 1840s. The tower was erected to give a good view across the River Avon.

72 The scene at Bathampton Weir looks peaceful on this early 20th-century postcard. Later, the spot became very busy with day trippers, the right-hand part of the mill building in the background bearing a huge sign, 'Weir Tea Gardens'.

BATHEASTON

73   This view of the River Avon and its surroundings shows Batheaston in the foreground with Bathford in the distance. To the north-west of Batheaston is high ground, climbing to a height of over 600ft, which is topped by Little Solisbury Camp, an Iron-Age fort.

74 Avondale Brewery, *c*.1904. In 1851, the brewery was run by the Emerson family. By 1881, Henry Morgan was maltster and brewer there. The Avondale Brewery was near the toll bridge over the River Avon.

BATH

75 Bath is surrounded by hills from which very fine views of the city and neighbouring countryside can be obtained. In this view of Bath from Beacon Hill, dating from *c*.1840, the River Avon can be seen winding through the city. At this time, the river, connecting with the Kennet & Avon Canal, was used for the transport of goods and it was part of the route, by water, from London to Bristol.

76 The Boating Station at Forester Road was operated by the Bath Boating Co. In 1927, this boat-building firm was advertising, 'All description of Boats, Punts and Canadian Canoes built to order and let on hire by hour or day.' Frederick Fisher was the proprietor of the Boating Station at this time. It was thought that the best and prettiest reaches of the river for boating were from Bath Boating Station to Warleigh via Bathampton Weir.

77 Cleveland Bridge, with its lodges built in the Greek Doric style, is the first bridge downriver from the Boating Station. This one-arched bridge, uniting Bathwick and Walcot, was designed by Henry Goodridge and built of cast iron in 1827. The scene looks tranquil in this old postcard view, but nowadays Cleveland Bridge carries a very busy road.

78 The next bridge downstream is Pulteney Bridge, built at the expense of Sir William Pulteney. Designed by Robert Adam, Pulteney Bridge was erected in the early 1770s. The three-arched bridge, with shops on either side, connects High Street and Great Pulteney Street. The background of this early 20th-century view shows Bath upriver of Pulteney Bridge.

79 This view of the south side of Pulteney Bridge shows projecting extensions, which are now long gone. The projection on the right of the bridge once advertised Roworth, watch maker and jeweller, while a sign above the shop, over the middle arch of the bridge, was an advertisement for Madame Hamilton, corset and belt maker. In 1914, William Roworth, watch maker, was at No. 10 Pulteney Bridge and Mrs Jane Hamilton, corset maker, was at No. 14. At that time, shops on the south side of bridge included two stationers, a tobacconist and a fruiterer. Pulteney Weir has undergone a change since this early 20th-century photograph was taken. Constructed in a rounded V-shape with three steps, a modern weir now enhances the setting of the renowned bridge.

80 At the time of Domesday, Bath Abbey had a mill on the River Avon. This was likely to have been in the same spot as the later Monks Mill shown in this engraving dating from *c.*1830. John Wood, in *An Essay towards a Description of Bath*, noted that Lot Lane led from the East Gate, close under the City Wall, to Monks Mill. The site of the mill is between Pulteney Bridge and North Parade Bridge.

81 A short distance downriver of Pulteney Bridge, the tall *Empire Hotel* was erected in 1901. The hotel offered breakfast for 3s., lunch for 3s. 6d. and dinner for 5s. 6d. Full terms in summer were five guineas per week. Despite its grandness, there were some who thought that the height of the building interfered with the architectural harmony of the city. This view of the riverside hotel, with Bath Abbey in the background, was taken *c*.1913.

82 The west front of Bath Abbey, 1864. The abbey church of St Peter and St Paul dates from the beginning of the 16th century. It was started by Oliver King, the Bishop of Bath and Wells, after the bishop's visitation to Bath in 1499. He is said to have had a dream in which the Holy Trinity appeared to him in the company of angels who were ascending and descending ladders. In his dream, Oliver King heard the words, 'Let an olive establish the crown and let a king restore the church.' Bath Abbey is noted for the two ladders, on either side of the great west window of seven lights, upon which angels are climbing.

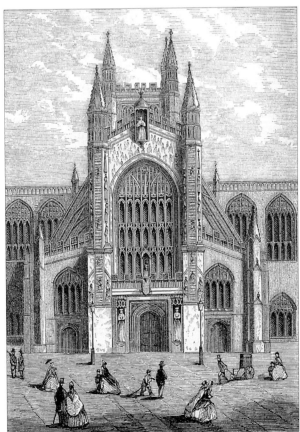

83 The Grand Pump Room (West End) and Baths, 1864. Over the centuries, Bath has been celebrated for its hot mineral springs. Taking the waters was a popular pastime among visitors to the city. The Grand Pump Room, situated on the south-west side of Abbey Churchyard, was erected in 1796 on the site of the former Pump Room, which was associated with Beau Nash, a famous Master of Ceremonies in 18th-century Bath.

PUMP ROOMS AND BATHS

☞ **VISITORS TO BATH ARE PARTICULARLY REQUESTED TO INSPECT THE BATHS,**
Which may be done free of Charge.

Terms for Drinking the Bath hot Mineral Waters.

One Week	..	£0	1	6	Six Months	..	£0	15	0
One Month	..	0	5	0	One Year	..		1	0	0
Three Months		0	10	0	A Family, One				
					Year	..		2	0	0

N.B.—If at the HETLING PUMP ROOM *exclusively*, 1s. per Week. No charge is made for tasting the Waters.

TIMES FOR DRINKING THE WATERS.

Week days—Eight a.m. to half-past Four p.m.
Sundays—At GRAND PUMP ROOM—Half-past Eight to half-past Nine a.m., and One to Three p.m.

The waters can be obtained in Half-pint Bottles, at 4s. per Dozen, by application to the Superintendent.

Terms for Bathing.
AT THE KING'S AND QUEEN'S BATHS.

From Six a.m. till Ten p.m. from Lady-day to Michaelmas
From Seven a.m. till Ten p.m. from Michaelmas to Lady-day
  First Class Bath, 1s. 6d.; Second Class Bath, 6d.; Ditto, with Fire, 1s.; Vapour Bath, 2s.; Shower Bath, 1s.; Vapour and Shower Bath combined, 2s. 6d.; First Class Douche, 1s.; Second Class Douche, 6d.; Pumping in the Bath, 6d.; One additional Bather in each Bath—First Class, 1s., Second Class, 6d.

DAYS FOR BATHING.

KING'S SIDE: *Gentlemen*—Monday, Wednesday, Friday.
      Ladies—Tuesday, Thursday, Saturday.
QUEEN'S SIDE: *Gentlemen*—Tuesday, Thursday, Saturday.
      Ladies—Monday, Wednesday, Friday.

These Baths are open on Sundays, from Seven to half-past Nine a.m., and One to Three p.m.

Baths may be taken at any Temperature to 115° Fahrenheit.

84 This advertisement for the Pump Room and Baths dates from 1864. It was included in *The Historic Guide to Bath* by the Rev. G.N. Wright, which was published in the same year. At this time, baths could also be taken in the Royal Baths, the Tepid Swimming Bath, the Hot Public Bath and the Cross Bath. The Tepid Swimming Bath had both private and public dressing rooms, but no bather was to occupy a dressing room for more than 40 minutes! The Hot Bath was free from 9 a.m. until noon for the use of 'the Poor', but the latter had to have a 'Certificate of a Resident Medical Practitioner countersigned by the Mayor or a Magistrate being a member of the Town Council'. The Cross Bath was for males only and the charge was 3d. with a towel, or 2d. if the bathers brought their own towels. The 'Portable Baths', filled with mineral waters at a temperature not exceeding 106 degrees, which could be supplied at any short distance, conjures up a fascinating picture.

85　Bath is famous for its baths, which were built in Roman times. The large rectangular Great Bath was discovered in the early 1880s. It is 82ft long, 40ft wide and open to the sky. Steps lead down into the water. Surrounding the Roman bath is a wide stone pavement, with seat recesses, and the bases upon which once stood huge pillars.

86　The vaulted fountain topped by an urn, which was once situated in Stall Street, was designed in 1859 by Stefano Pieroni. It gave a free supply of the mineral water for which Bath was renowned. This view of the fountain dates from *c*.1909.

87 Situated on an incline, Milsom Street was originally erected in the 1760s as a residential neighbourhood. However, this busy scene, dating from *c*.1908, shows its transformation into a street of fashionable shops and banks.

88 The Circus, designed by John Wood the elder, has three entrances, one at Gay Street, another at Brock Street and a third at Bennett Street. It is noted for the three classic orders on the facade of the buildings. The ground floor is Doric, while the first floor is Ionic and the second floor is Corinthian. Among the famous people associated with The Circus are William Pitt, Earl of Chatham, who lived at No. 7 from 1755-63, and Thomas Gainsborough, the portrait painter, who resided at No. 24 in 1770.

89 The Royal Crescent, the work of John Wood the younger, was erected in 1769 in the Ionic style of architecture. Overlooking the River Avon, it is the largest of the crescents in Bath and comprises 30 houses. Christopher Anstey, author of a volume of verse entitled the *New Bath Guide*, lived at No. 5 in 1770, while No. 9 was the residence of Edward Bulwer, Lord Lytton, in 1866. Sir Isaac Pitman, a long-time inhabitant of Bath and the inventor of shorthand, died here in January 1897.

90 A marble bust of Sir Isaac Pitman was among busts of other notable figures in The Bath Royal Literary and Scientific Institution, in Terrace Walk. The institution, shown on the right of this view, was built in the Doric style during the 1820s on the site of the old Assembly Rooms, which had burnt down. It had a library and a museum containing Roman antiquities and a natural history collection. In the building, there was also a reading room where both London and provincial newspapers could be read, a room where chess was played and a lecture hall. The institute no longer stands, having been demolished during road improvements.

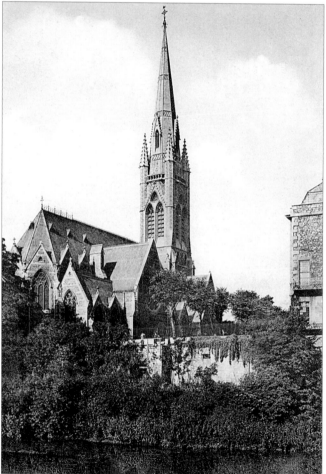

91 The Bath Royal Literary and Scientific Institution was not far from North Parade Bridge. This single-arched cast iron bridge was built, in 1835, to the plans of William Tierney Clark of London, who also designed Hammersmith Bridge and Marlow Bridge. Just over 100 years later, the ironwork of the North Parade Bridge was encased with stone.

92 A short distance downstream of North Parade Bridge and situated in South Parade is the 19th-century Roman Catholic church of St John the Evangelist. Designed by architect Charles Hansom of Clifton, its tower and tall spire attain a height of over 200ft. The church was consecrated on 6 October 1863.

93 This steel engraving, dating from *c*.1845, shows a train crossing the Skew Bridge to Bath's Great Western Railway station. A pair of narrowboats is breasted up against the towpath, while the boat horse waits patiently. Downstream, the Old Bridge can be seen through the arches of the railway bridge.

94 Old Bridge, *c*.1907. In times past, after North Parade Bridge, the five-arched Old Bridge, at the end of Southgate Street, was the next road bridge to cross the river. Originally constructed in the 14th century, the bridge was once known as St Laurence's Bridge. It connected the city with the parish of Widcombe and Lyncombe. The Old Bridge no longer exists. Traffic now crosses the River Avon via Churchill Bridge.

95 Southgate Street, *c*.1920. The road, over the Old Bridge, leading into the main shopping centre of Bath, looks fairly quiet in this view with just two trams and a horse-drawn vehicle. However, on Saturdays, in particular, during the early years of the 20th century, this thoroughfare was often thronged with people. Among the local citizens were also Clifton and Bristol folk who would often go to Bath just for the shopping.

96 Old Bridge and Beechen Cliff, *c*.1920s. A favourite walk, in times past, was up to Beechen Cliff, which is in the background of this view. Here, fine views over the city and surrounding countryside could be obtained. After crossing either the Old Bridge or the footbridge behind the Great Western Railway station, walkers could ascend by the Holloway. Alternatively, they could take a tram on the Combe Down route, as far as the *Bear Inn*, and then walk the rest of the way.

New Bridge

97 The title of this old print, dating from *c*.1840, is 'Weston Bridge, near Bath'. Presumably, it was given this title as the elegant stone bridge, with a single arch, was erected on the southern boundary of the parish of Weston. Ernest Walls, in *The Bristol Avon*, called it Newton Bridge and described it as 'the most handsome of the bridges crossing the Avon'. It is now generally known as New Bridge.

Saltford

98 Clifton Rowing Club Boathouse, *c*.1911. In the early years of the 20th century, boating was a popular pastime on the river at Saltford. The Saltford Regatta, in which rowing clubs competed against each other, was held here from 1890 to 1972. It was one of the social as well as sporting events of the year in the neighbourhood.

99 *Arrowsmith's Dictionary of Bristol*, published in 1906, observed that the majority of the members of the Clifton Rowing Club were inclined to devote themselves to boating rather than to serious rowing. However, the club had recently revived rowing among its members and it was hoped that these efforts would be continued. Then, the subscription to the club was £1 11s. 6d. annually, with an entrance fee of 10s. 6d.

100 At Saltford, in 1914, rowing boats, punts and canoes could be hired from two premises, Withey's Boat Hiring Station, run by George Withey, and Sheppard's Boathouse, operated by George Sheppard. Both venues had tea rooms. Saltford was easily reached by train and thousands of visitors came annually to this delightful riverside location.

101 This view, looking over the river from Saltford, dates from the early 1900s. It shows Kelston Lock and weir and the chimneys of the annealing furnaces of Saltford's 18th-century brass mill. Disused by 1924, the mill was restored in the mid-1990s.

102 It was not only boating that attracted visitors to Saltford. These young men had cycled to Saltford from Bristol to swim in the river. Ted Tavernder, Raymond Thompson and George Thompson sat on one of the balance beams at Saltford Lock for this photograph, taken *c*.1936. The plus fours and the patterned socks worn by the Thompson brothers were all the rage among cyclists at that time.

103 The two chimneys of the annealing furnaces of Kelston Brass Mill can be seen from Saltford Lock. The mill was in use, up to the end of the 1840s, as a battery mill where the metal was beaten with a hammer to shape it.

BITTON

104 Part of the ancient church of St Mary dates from Norman times, while its fine Perpendicular tower was built in the 14th century. Next to the church is The Grange, formerly the parsonage, which dates from at least the 13th century or perhaps even earlier. The 16th-century Dower House is on the right of the picture.

105 Paper making started at Bitton, during the 1830s, in a mill on the bank of the River Boyd, a tributary of the River Avon. In *The History of Kingswood Forest* (1891), the Rev. J.A. Braine wrote about the extensive paper mills of Messrs. Sommerville, which had been enlarged and rebuilt in 1876. Writing 15 years later, the author noted, 'Here are about 400 hands employed manufacturing nearly forty tons of the finest writing paper per week for the Government.'

106   The old three-arched County Bridge, which once crossed the Avon at Keynsham, separated the county of Gloucestershire from that of Somerset. A stone seat, known as the Abbot's Chair, was built into one of the walls in the middle of the bridge. Anyone who sat there could have one foot in Gloucestershire and the other in Somerset. The great flood of 1968 destroyed the County Bridge and it was replaced by a new bridge.

107   Dating from the 13th century, the parish church of Keynsham is dedicated to St John the Baptist. In 1632, there was a tremendous thunderstorm, which caused the tower to collapse. Originally at the east end of the north aisle, the tower was rebuilt at the western end of the church in 1634. Restored between 1861 and 1863, the church has a number of interesting features. These include carved wooden screens, a 17th-century pulpit, an early 18th-century font and monuments to Sir Henry Bridges who died in 1587 and to Sir Thomas Bridges who died in 1661.

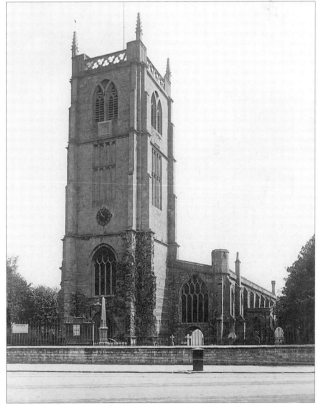

108 High Street, Keynsham, *c.*1903. The shop with the lamps at either side of the door, on the extreme left of this view, was once kept by ironmonger, John Down. Later, it was run by Robert Hickling. On the right is the Baptist Church with its decorative gate, overhead lamp and ornamental railings. Next to this place of worship was the Post Office at 37 High Street. Miss Rachel Spiller was postmistress in the 1880s and, as Mrs Harvey, she ran the premises in the early 1900s.

109 Pleasure steamers from Bristol usually turned at Keynsham Lock before making the return trip downriver. The bottom gates of the lock stand open in this view, which possibly dates from the 1920s. The lock keeper's brick-built shelter, with its tall chimney, can be seen on the lock side, while in the background, along the weir stream, is the old County Bridge.

110　Londonderry Wharf, *c.*1910. Coal from Gloucestershire collieries was once transported along the Dramway to Londonderry Wharf to be carried to its final destination by water. The Dramway, a branch of the Avon & Gloucestershire Railway, was built in 1833. It had fallen into decline by the 1860s, but was opened again in the early 1880s to take coal from the California Pit at Oldland where a new deep shaft had been sunk. The transport of Oldland coal to the wharf stopped when the California Pit was flooded in 1904. In the first half of the 20th century, the wharf became known locally as 'Jack White's Corner' as the occupants of the cottage, on the right of this view, were Keynsham lock keeper, Jack White, and his wife, Sarah. The narrowboat in the middle of the river, with four ropes securing it to both banks, may possibly have been a spoon dredger.

HANHAM

111　The smaller building, in the centre of this view at Hanham Mills, was once the *Chequers Inn*. It is now known as the *Old Lock and Weir*. The larger building, on the right, took the name of the *Chequers Inn*, when it was erected in the early 20th century.

112   Rowing boats are moored, at the bend of the river by the *Chequers Inn*, in this view of Hanham Mills, dating from *c*.1913. Nowadays, there are visitor moorings for pleasure craft using the river. As there are two public houses here, it is a busy spot during the summer months.

113   Below the weir at Hanham Mills, the tow ropes of a pair of horse-drawn narrowboats were being sorted out before the boats continued their journey downstream to Bristol. As the towing path for horses was around the side of the weir, rather than the lock, a narrowboat would be shafted out of the lock and the river current would be utilised to reach the opposite bank where the boat horse and horse marine would be waiting.

114   Bees' Tea Gardens, established in 1846 opposite Conham, was a favourite place for day-trippers crossing the river via Conham Ferry or coming up from Bristol in pleasure boats. This picture postcard of the riverside gardens dates from *c*.1904. Locally known as Beese's Tea Gardens, the premises are still in existence and are a popular venue for boating parties.

115   In this view, dating from *c*.1906, a marquee has been erected by Bees' Tea Gardens and a steamer has come upriver from Bristol. Obviously, an interesting event is taking place, judging by the crowd gathered on the Conham side of the river.

116   The Ariel Rowing Club Boathouse, on the St Anne's bank of the river, would have been an interesting sight for boating parties on a steamer trip upriver from Bristol. Its large boathouse was equipped with a fleet of boats for all classes of rowing and there was a separate building for pleasure boats and a tea-house. This old picture postcard view looks across from the St George side of the river and dates from *c*.1907.

BRISTOL

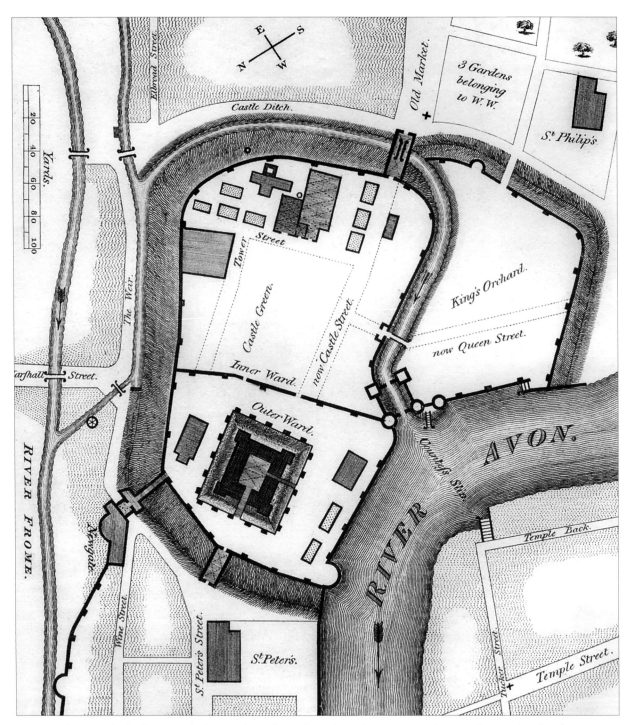

117 Robert, Earl of Gloucester, built Bristol Castle in the early 12th century on the site of an earlier fortification. It covered an area of about six acres and the great stone keep is said to have been inferior in size only to the White Tower at London and Colchester Castle. The castle was destroyed by the order of Oliver Cromwell in 1655. This map of Bristol Castle is from Samuel Seyer's *Memoirs Historical and Topographical of Bristol and its Neighbourhood*, in which the author wrote: 'Strong and spacious as it was for almost 600 years, it has now disappeared; its memory is preserved by the names of *Castle-street*, *Castle-green*, *Castle-ditch*, and *Castle Precincts*; and those who dwell in any part of its site, still describe themselves as living *in the Castle*.'

118 St Peter's Hospital was near both the castle and the river. The original ancient building belonged to the Norton family, but was extensively renovated in the early 17th century by merchant, Robert Aldworth. In 1698, the premises were purchased by the Corporation and made into a workhouse for the poor. Six hundred paupers were resident there at the time of the 1832 cholera outbreak, when 58 girls slept in 10 beds and 70-80 boys shared 18 beds. Not surprisingly, the disease was virulent here at this time. St Peter's Hospital, one of the most attractive buildings in the old city, was lost in the bombing of Bristol during the Second World War.

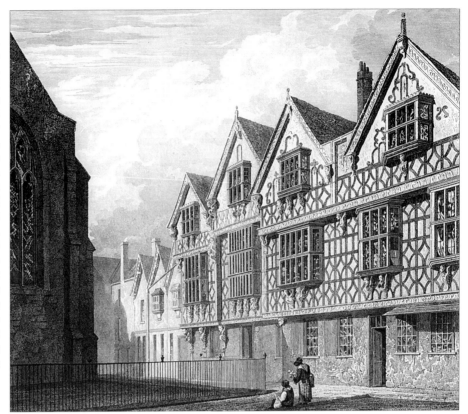

119 The former Bristol Bridge had three stone piers and four stone arches. Its houses projected over the water from the dark and narrow passageway of the bridge. The first step into a shop was on the timbers of the ground floor. This was all that was between one's feet and the water and it was very draughty when the wind blew through the crevices! A parlour and a kitchen were usually on the first floor and two bedchambers were on each of the second and third floors. Two garrets were on the fourth floor, while some houses had leaden platforms making five floors in all. The bridge was a crowded thoroughfare so it was a good place for trade. Many wealthy tradesmen lived here and the houses, built of wood, were let at the highest rents in the city.

120   Old Bristol Bridge was taken down and replaced by a new bridge. John Morgan's *A Brief Historical Sketch of Bristol with the New Picture of Clifton, and Stranger's Guide* gave the following description of its successor:

The principal entrance into the City of Bristol is over the Bridge from Bath Street and Redcliffe Street ... it was finished and opened on the 17th. of September, 1768; is built of hewn stone, brought from the quarries of Courtfield, bordering on the River Wye, Monmouthshire and consists of three circular arches; their piers are forty-two feet long, and ten feet thick, the span of the centre arch is fifty feet, the two side arches are thirty-nine feet each: it has balustrades of Portland stone seven feet high, and a raised footpath on either side ... At each end are two freestone buildings formerly used for the collection of tolls, but now converted into retail shops.

121   Bristol Bridge, St Nicholas' Church and High Street, *c.*1908. The eastern part of the ancient church, which once stood here, was built upon St Nicholas' Gate. This was one of the boundaries of the city, the road from Bristol Bridge formerly passing under an archway. When the gate was removed, in 1762, part of the old church had to be demolished. It was decided that a new church should be erected in its place and this was finished in 1768. The Georgian church suffered extensive damage during the Blitz and many other buildings in this view were destroyed at this time.

122   The Tolsey, in Corn Street, once served as a place for transacting business, but this was superseded by the Exchange, which was designed by Bath architect, John Wood the elder, and opened in 1743. The Exchange is shown on the right in this view of Corn Street, dating from *c*.1875. Outside the Exchange can be seen the famous Nails. These are brass tables, which were once outside the old Tolsey and used by merchants when making payments. The custom is said to have given rise to the phrase to 'pay down on the nail'. Dates inscribed on three of the Nails are 1594, 1625, and 1631. The one, which is said to be the oldest, is undated.

123   The former Guildhall is on the left of this view of Broad Street, which was included in Samuel Seyer's *Memoirs Historical and Topographical of Bristol and its Neighbourhood*. The recess between the tall pointed Guildhall windows contained a statue of Charles II. At the Guildhall, the sessions for the City and County of Bristol were held. There were rooms in it for the sheriff's court and a hall, called St George's Chapel, in which the city officers were appointed annually and the county members chosen. In the background of the picture can be seen the church of St John the Baptist with its ancient gateway. This church once formed part of the town wall, its belfry tower and spire having been erected over one of the main gateways to the city.

124 Left: Quarter Jacks and the Dutch House, Bristol, *c.*1920. Christ Church with St Ewen, opened in 1790, is situated at the corner of Wine Street and Broad Street on the site of an ancient church demolished in 1787. The Quarter Jacks, standing ready to swing their hammers against the bells on either side of the church clock, were from the original building. In times past, the tall half-timbered Dutch House stood at the corner of High Street and Wine Street. Over the centuries, it had been used as a dwelling, a bank and a shop. In 1908, the City Council decided that it should be renovated, to facilitate street improvement, rather than be demolished. Subsequently, the shop front was cut back to obtain a wider pavement and slender columns were used to support the upper storeys, which were overhanging. Sadly, the historic 17th-century Dutch House was severely damaged on 24 November 1940, during the Blitz. Shortly afterwards, it was pulled down by soldiers whose task was to make the streets safe.

125 Below left: Wine Street was one of the four chief streets of the old city, the others being High Street, Broad Street and Corn Street. Formerly known as Wynch Street, the pillory was set up here, where offenders, with their heads and hands stuck through holes in the boards, were pelted with rotten eggs or produce. Wine Street's claim to fame was that Robert Southey, the poet, was born on 12 August 1774 at No. 9. This print of the street dates from 1875. At that time, and for years to come, Wine Street was noted for its drapers. Eight drapery establishments were there in 1875, plus four hosiers. During the Second World War, Wine Street suffered bomb damage and was destroyed along with other parts of old Bristol.

126 Below: The Welsh Back, below Bristol Bridge, was a popular place for laying up boats. Barges, narrowboats and trows were moored against each other when this photograph, dating from *c.*1906, was taken from Bristol Bridge. At this time, the Cardigan & Carmarthen S. S. Carriers and R. Burton & Son, Ltd, Steam Ship Carriers, operated from the Welsh Back. The building, on the extreme right, was the school and warehouse of the Smith Premier Type Writer Co. Further down, were the premises of tobacco and snuff manufacturers, leather factors, biscuit makers, wholesale fruit importers, ironfounders, corn merchants, hide merchants and wine and spirit merchants. The *Golden Bottle*, the *Cross Keys*, the *White Hart* and the *Bell* were among the other buildings along the Welsh Back.

127   Welsh Back looking towards Bristol Bridge in the early
years of the 20th century. This view changed dramatically
during the Second World War, when buildings in Back Bridge
Street, on the far side of the bridge, were bombed.

128   The famous Bristol inn, the *Llandoger Trow*, in King
Street, just off Welsh Back, was formerly called the *Llandoger
Tavern* or sometimes the *Llandoger*. It derives its name
from Llandogo, in Monmouthshire, whence great quantities
of bark and timber were once shipped to Bristol aboard
sailing vessels called trows. This illustration of the inn at
5 King Street dates from *c*.1881 when Thomas Daniel was its
proprietor. Originally one of a group of five timber-framed
houses erected in 1664, the inn survived the Blitz of 1940 when
two of the houses were destroyed. The three remaining gabled
houses now form the premises of the *Llandoger Trow*.

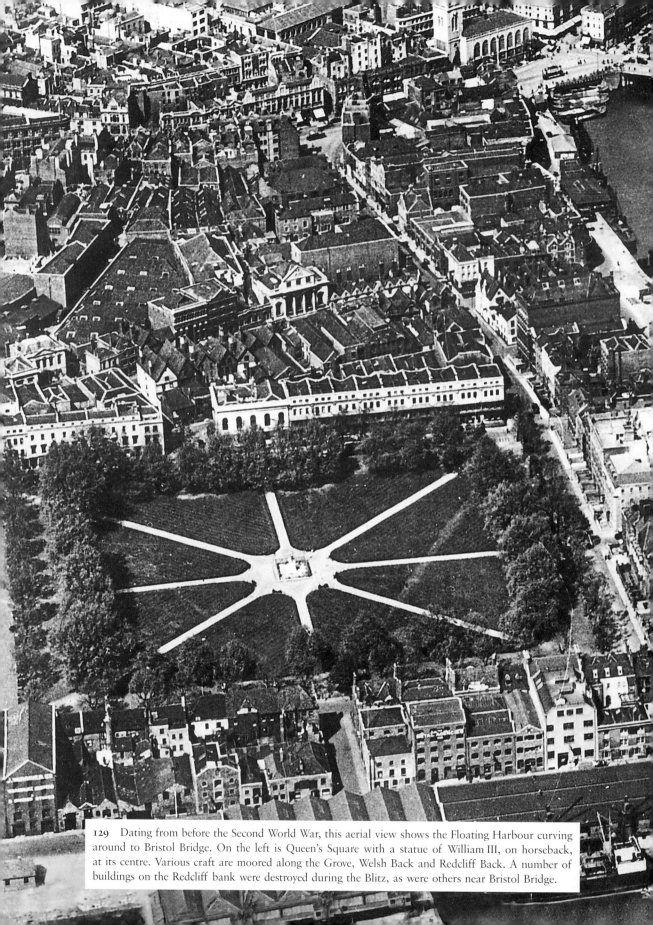

129 Dating from before the Second World War, this aerial view shows the Floating Harbour curving around to Bristol Bridge. On the left is Queen's Square with a statue of William III, on horseback, at its centre. Various craft are moored along the Grove, Welsh Back and Redcliff Back. A number of buildings on the Redcliff bank were destroyed during the Blitz, as were others near Bristol Bridge.

Great Western Steamship Line.

BRISTOL AND NEW YORK.

SOMERSET	...	...	2000 Tons	...	...	WM. WESTERN, Commander.
CORNWALL	...	...	2000 "	...	...	WM. STAMPER, "
ARRAGON	...	...	1500 "	...	...	GEORGE SYMONS, "

The Vessels of this Line carry only a limited number of Passengers, every attention being paid to their comfort and convenience.

RATES OF PASSAGE.

SALOON.—Thirteen Guineas for each Adult ; Children under twelve years, 21s. per year ; Infants, One Guinea. Return Tickets available for twelve calendar months from date of issue, Twenty Guineas.

These Rates include a liberal Table, without Wines or Liquors, which can be obtained on board

£5 deposit is required to secure Saloon Berths, the balance to be paid before sailing. No charge for Steward's Fee.

SECOND CABIN Passage to New York, Boston, or Philadelphia, Eight Guineas ; Children under eight, half fare ; Infants under twelve months, one Guinea.

Second Cabin Passengers are provided with Beds, Bedding, and all necessary Utensils, Wash Basins, &c., and with a good Dietary Table.

STEERAGE Passage to New York, Boston, or Philadelphia, including an abundant supply of cooked Provisions, Five Guineas.

Passengers booked through to all parts of the United States and Canada on very moderate terms in connection with the Erie Railway Company.

Twenty Cubic Feet of Luggage will be allowed for each Adult Saloon Passenger, Fifteen Cubic Feet for each Adult Second Cabin, and Ten feet for each Steerage Passenger free ; for over that quantity a charge of 1s. 6d. for each Cubic Foot will be made.

Goods carried at moderate rates of freight, which may be paid either here or in America. The Shippers to bear all risks of lighterage, river-craft and fire.

For Freight or Passage apply, in NEW YORK, to W. D. MORGAN, 70, South Street ; in HAVRE, to J. M. CURRIE ; in BORDEAUX, to CURRIE & Co., 19, Ruy Foy ; in LONDON, to DONALD CURRIE & Co., 3 and 4, Fenchurch Street ; in MANCHESTER, F. W. STOREY, 17, Tickinson Street ; in BIRMINGHAM, C. W. MILNE, 16 and 17, Exchange Buildings, in HALIFAX, to JOHN EVISON, 40, Commercial Road ; in SOUTHAMPTON, to H. MILLER, 34, Oxford Street ; in DERBY to JOHN BRATBY & Co., 27, Bold Lane ; in PLYMOUTH, to SANDERS STEVENS, & Co., Exchange ; and in BRISTOL, to the Managers,

MARK WHITWILL & SON,
GROVE AVENUE, QUEEN SQUARE.

130 The firm of Mark Whitwill & Son, steam and sailing ship brokers, insurance and commission agents, was established in 1831. By 1893, Mark Whitwill & Son were the managers of the Great Western Steamship Line as well as being agents for steamers from Bristol to Glasgow and Belfast for both passengers and cargo. On occasion, they acted as cargo agents for vessels loading at Bristol for Melbourne and Sydney. The firm also represented a number of other shipping companies and transacted business in booking passengers and emigrants to all parts of the world over the shortest routes. Emigrants to the United States of America could board ship at Bristol. The advertisement for the Great Western Steamship Line, shown here, dates from 1875.

131 This view of the Great Crane, in the late 18th century, was included in *The History and Antiquities of the City of Bristol* by William Barrett. The author wrote:

To land the goods with greater dispatch, several cranes are erected on the Wharf of the Quay at proper distances; that built and contrived by the ingenious Mr. Padmore, by the Mud-dock, near the Gibb, is an excellent piece of mechanism, fixed on large pillars of wood, and underneath it the goods are secured from the weather.

132 The truncated spire of St Mary Redcliffe Church was a familiar sight to Bristolians for over 400 years. A great part of the tall spire had been destroyed by a terrible storm of thunder and lightning at St Paul's tide, in 1445, when the roof, part of the nave and the southern aisle were also damaged. Despite the lack of the spire, Elizabeth I, on her visit to St Mary Redcliffe in 1574, declared the church to be, 'the fairest, the goodliest and most famous parish church in England.' In the foreground, of this view, which dates from c.1842, sailing ships lie at anchor in the Floating Harbour, while a small rowing boat crosses the stretch of water.

133 The Floating Harbour from Prince Street Bridge. The tall spire of St Mary Redcliffe Church can be seen on the right of this pre-1918 old postcard view. It became the second highest spire in the country when it was rebuilt in 1872, to a height of 292ft. In the far distance is Redcliffe Wharf, while Midland Wharf is to the right of the picture. Besides the rowing boat in the foreground, a variety of craft can be seen. Sailing vessels are in the background, while the steam tug, *Ariel*, is on the right. A railway-owned barge is moored next to the open-fronted shed on the left.

134 In this pre-1914 view of the Floating Harbour, the trow, *Taff*, is on the right of the picture. Trows were flat-bottomed sailing craft, which operated on the Rivers Avon and Severn and also in the Bristol Channel. Colin Green, in *Severn Traders* (1999), noted that this iron trow was one of four, which were constructed in 1860 by Hyde & Rowe of Bristol for the firm of Danks, Venn & Co.

135 In the mid-19th century, only two public bridges, Bedminster Bridge and Bath Bridge, spanned the New Cut. These iron structures were rebuilt during the second half of the 19th century. By the end of the first decade of the 20th century, besides railway bridges, other bridges spanning the New Cut included Netham Bridge, Totterdown Bridge, Langton Street Footbridge, Vauxhall Footbridge and Ashton Swing Bridge, which was both a road and railway bridge. Men and boys at Bedminster Bridge watch the photographer in this peaceful scene dating from *c*.1906. There are only two vehicles in sight, a tram on the bridge, advertising Ogden's cigarettes, and a horse-drawn conveyance climbing Redcliff Hill. The *George & Dragon*, on the left of this view, was kept by Walter James in 1901 and by Mary Frank in 1906.

136 Bathurst Basin Lock and General Hospital, *c.*1906. The entrance to Bathurst Basin from the New Cut was through Bathurst Lock. This lock was sealed up at the beginning of the Second World War to prevent the water in the Floating Harbour draining in the event of bomb damage. The Bristol General Hospital was founded in 1832, but the building shown in this view dates from 1858. Designed by architect, W.B. Gingell, in a style that became known as 'Bristol Byzantine', the hospital formed three sides of a quadrangle, its tall octagonal tower topped by a cupola. This distinctive dome was destroyed during the Blitz.

137 Bristolians, crowded aboard the four-masted German barque *H. Hackfield*, were waiting for the arrival of King Edward VII and Queen Alexandra at St Augustine's Bridge on 9 July 1908. This was the day when the king and queen visited Bristol during the morning and opened the Royal Edward Dock at Avonmouth in the afternoon.

138 Electric tramways were first used in Bristol in 1895. They carried on until 1941. This view of the Tramway Centre dates from *c*.1906. At this time, an average journey of a mile could be made on any of the tram routes for a penny. On the left of the picture, the ship with a tall funnel is moored by the Dublin Shed and the newly erected C.W.S. building overlooks St Augustine's Reach. E Shed, with its dome, is on the right, while the lofty masts of sailing ships are in the background.

139 In the past, a drawbridge over the River Frome allowed craft to pass further along the Floating Harbour. The bridge, built in 1714, was replaced by another in 1755. The latter was raised 'by a curious subterranean, mechanical contrivance of iron wheels with cogs' requiring two people on either side to elevate it. It was superseded by another structure, erected in 1827. This had a carriage way, which was 18ft wide with a 5ft-wide footpath on either side. In 1868, it was replaced by the final drawbridge over the Frome. Opening the drawbridge caused great interruption to traffic so, just over 20 years later, the end of the Floating Harbour was covered over and a fixed bridge was opened here in 1893. The view was taken before 1878 as St Werburgh's Church, with its single turret, was taken down at that date.

140   The name of the pleasure steamer moored against the quayside is unknown, but those of the middle steamer and the one on the outside are just discernible as *Kate* and *Emily*. Sailing craft add interest to this photograph of the end of St Augustine's Reach, which dates from *c*.1908.

141   'Coastwise and continental lines of shipping' are shown in this view of St Augustine's Reach, dating from the 1920s. Cargoes are piled on Narrow Quay, which is to the right of the picture. Bush House, on the extreme right, was originally built about 1830 as a tea warehouse. It is now the Arnolfini, a centre for contemporary arts.

142 Samuel Seyer included this portrait of Sebastian Cabot in his *Memoirs Historical and Topographical of Bristol and its Neighbourhood*. Sebastian Cabot was the son of John Cabot, a merchant and mariner, whose origins are said to be in Genoa, but who was also associated with Venice. It seems likely that the Cabot family settled in Bristol between 1494 and 1495. Letters patent were granted to John Cabot and his three sons by Henry VII on 5 March 1496, for the discovery of new and unknown lands. Cabot's ship, the *Matthew*, left Bristol in May 1497. It is possible that Sebastian sailed with his father, but this is not known for certain. After crossing the Atlantic Ocean, landfall was made on 24 June 1497.

143 Cabot Tower, crowning the summit of Brandon Hill, was built to commemorate the sighting and discovery of the continent of North America, in 1497, by John Cabot who sailed across the Atlantic in a Bristol ship crewed by Bristol seamen. Designed by W.V. Gough, the construction of Cabot Tower was started in 1897, the fourth centenary of this important event. The opening ceremony was on 6 September 1898. The 105ft-high tower is built of red sandstone and has dressings of Bath freestone. On the apex of its truncated spire is a figure representing Commerce, mounted on a globe, which symbolises the world. Ornamental balconies on two stages serve as viewpoints for a superb panorama of the city and its surroundings.

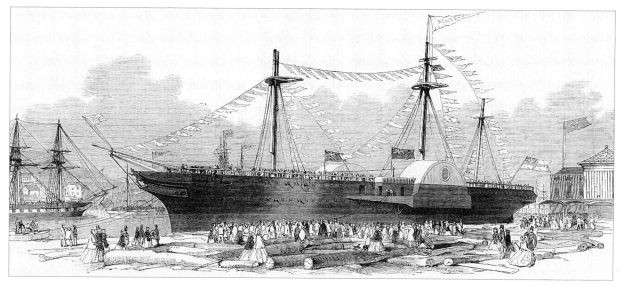

144 The launch of the *Demerara*, a Royal Mail steamship, took place at Bristol in 1851. She had been constructed by William Patterson, the builder of the steamships *Great Western* and *Great Britain*. The occasion was reported in the *Illustrated London News* of 4 October 1851, which featured this illustration of the vessel. At that time, with the exception of the *Great Britain*, the *Demerara* was said to be the largest steamship afloat. Her length overall was 316ft 3in. The extreme width from the outside of the paddle boxes was 72ft 5in. Built of British oak, teak and pine, the depth to the main deck was 26ft 8in, while the depth to the spar deck was 34ft. Tonnage was 3,126 tons. Unfortunately, after being towed by a tug at a fast pace down the Avon, the *Demerara* struck the Gloucestershire bank and was grounded on her maiden voyage. She was so badly damaged that she was turned into a sailing vessel and renamed. Her carved wooden figurehead of an African chief was saved and, for many years after, it was a feature on the wall of Demerara House at Quay Head on the corner of Quay Street and Rupert Street.

145 H.M.S. *Daedalus*, at Mardyke Ferry, *c.*1904. The old frigate, *Daedalus*, was sent to Bristol in 1861 to be used as a naval training ship. A claim to fame of the *Daedalus* was that, when she was in the South Atlantic in 1848, a 'sea serpent' was observed from the frigate. The captain drew a sketch of the creature, which was subsequently used as the basis for an illustration of the incident in *The Illustrated London News*. It was thought that about 60ft of the creature was visible, while 30-40ft of its length remained under water. At Bristol, the *Daedalus* was moored in the Floating Harbour and, in Edwardian times, she was serving as the drill ship for both the Royal Naval Artillery Volunteers and the Royal Navy Reserve.

146 Although, at the beginning of the 20th century, large ships were being accommodated at Avonmouth Docks, the City Docks were still lively. This view of the western end of the City Docks dates from c.1913. On the right is the timber yard by the Baltic Wharf. Other wharves further along, on the south shore of the Floating Harbour, included Onega, Cumberland, Canada, Gefle and Chatham. In the centre of the picture is the Hydraulic Engine House at Underfall Yard, with its tower and chimney stack. Hydraulic power was supplied to a variety of installations in the City Docks including locks and swing bridges.

147 Constructed of red brick in 1906, 1908 and 1919, the three tobacco bonded warehouses became a dominant feature of the City Docks. Imported tobacco was stored in these nine-storeyed buildings before duty was paid on it. Two further tobacco bonded warehouses were erected at Canon's Marsh in the 1920s, but they were built of reinforced concrete. Tobacco sampling at one of the warehouses is shown in this view dating from c.1924.

148 This photograph of the three-masted sailing vessel, *Arizona*, at Cumberland Basin was probably taken in the late 19th century. To the right of the picture is the *Pilot Hotel*, which was kept by Henry Hale in 1881 and by Thomas Tonkin in 1891.

149 This print, dating from *c.*1842, shows the entrance to Cumberland Basin from the tidal Avon. William Jessop's north entrance lock is on the left, while his smaller south entrance lock is on the right. The original Rownham Ferry is shown to the left of the view. This ferry was said to have been in operation since monastic times, when the abbot of St Augustine's Abbey used the crossing to gain access to his house in Abbot's Leigh. The ferry had to be repositioned, upstream, when a new entrance lock was later built at Cumberland Basin.

150 A paddle steamer manoeuvres in front of the entrance to the City Docks in this view dating from *c.*1910. On the left is the lock known as Howard's Lock after Thomas Howard whose plans for Cumberland Basin were put into action in 1872-3. To the right are the remains of Jessop's Lock, while further to the right is the Brunel Lock, built between 1844 and 1849 to replace the south entrance lock.

151 Ashton Swing Bridge, between Cumberland Basin and Ashton, was opened in October 1906. The lower deck of the bridge carried two railway lines, while the upper deck had a road, which was 20ft in width. On either side of the road, the footpath was 5ft 6in wide. The overall length of the bridge was about 600ft. This bridge could also swing open to allow the passage of masted craft up or down river. The movable section of the bridge was 202ft long and weighed about 1,000 tons. It was swung around by hydraulic engines operated from the cabin constructed over the bridge.

152 Clifton Bridge railway station, on the Somerset side of the River Avon, was on the line from Bristol to Portishead, which opened in April 1867. It originally belonged to the Bristol and Portishead Pier and Railway Company. Stations on the line were Clifton Bridge, Pill, Portbury, Portishead and Portishead Pier. Clifton Bridge railway station closed in September 1964.

153 Samuel Seyer included this illustration of the River Avon in his *Memoirs Historical and Topographical of Bristol and its Neighbourhood*. The engraving was intended to show the location of the ancient British station, Caer-Odor, at Clifton, on the right-hand side of the Avon Gorge where the Observatory now stands. The ruins of the old windmill, which was to become the Observatory, can be seen on the height.

154 Approach to the Hotwell House, *c.*1795. The medicinal waters at Hotwells, rising from a spring at a temperature of 76 degrees Fahrenheit, were much favoured in the 18th century. By 1789, so many buildings had been built in Hotwells that, in *The History and Antiquities of the City of Bristol*, William Barrett wrote: 'And the buildings lately erected there give it more the appearance of a large town than of lodgings, for the sick alone, and have so increased of late as to join the Hotwells quite to Bristol, by an uninterrupted chain of houses.'

155 In 1789, William Barret used this engraving of Hotwells in *The History and Antiquities of the City of Bristol* and remarked:

On St Augustine's side of the city, a mile down the river Avon, is the noted rock of St Vincent, which furnishes the naturalist with those beautiful pieces of spar called Bristol stones, and other fossils, corals and shells, and the more noted fountain of Hotwell water, issuing from the bottom of the rock which has given to the place the name HOTWELL.

156 *New York City*, Hotwells. At the beginning of the 20th century, there were ten steamships in the Bristol City Line, which traded from Bristol to New York, including one named *New York City*. Four Bristol City Line ships bore the name of *New York City*. The first was an iron ship of 1,725 tons built by Richardson, Duck & Company of Stockton-on-Tees in 1879. The second, at 2,970 tons, was made of steel and built by Richardson in 1907. The third, a steel ship of 2,736 tons, was built by Charles Hill & Sons in 1917. The fourth, a steel ship of 7,052 tons, was bought secondhand and joined the fleet in 1951. The second *New York City* is shown in this view.

157 *City of Cologne*, Hotwells, *c*.1910. This postcard was sent to his son by a father who was about to travel possibly on this very ship. Dating the card, 'Bristol 22.3.10', the sender wrote, 'Sailing tomorrow morning for Hamburg. Hope to have a fine run and to hear from you on arrival Sunday.'

158 In the past, Bristol Channel paddle steamers were a familiar sight on the River Avon at Hotwells. Excursions would run from Bristol down the Somerset coast or over to South Wales. P. & A. Campbell Ltd ran the White Funnel Fleet from Bristol, but there were rival paddle steamer businesses, which operated from the Welsh ports of Swansea, Barry and Cardiff.

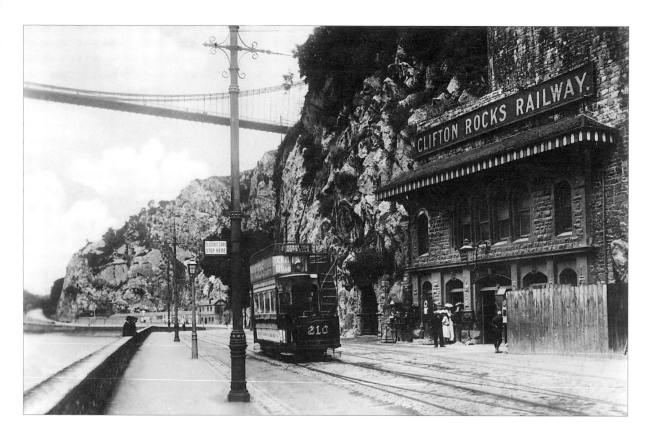

159 The Clifton Rocks Railway opened in 1893 and ran between Hotwells and Sion Hill until 1934. Initially, this funicular railway, built inside the cliffs of the Avon Gorge, was a great attraction for visitors. About a hundred thousand passengers were carried up or down within the first six weeks of the opening when the fare was 'a penny up and a ha'penny down'. By 1906, the fare was 2d. up and 1d. down, but through tickets were issued on the Hotwells section of the tramway at 2d. from the Tramway Centre to the top of the Clifton Rocks Railway.

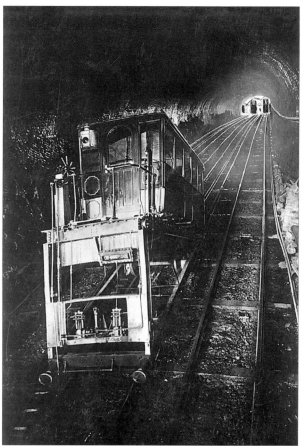

160 The steeply sloping 450ft-long tunnel for the Clifton Rocks Railway took several years to excavate, through the rocks, and had a gradient of about 1 in 2. The four cars inside the tunnel were worked in pairs connected by steel cables. They were drawn up and down the rails by water power. Water was used as ballast in the car going down, which made it heavier than the car at the bottom. As the upper car descended, it pulled the lower car up the slope. At the end of a journey, the water was pumped back to the top.

161 A short distance beyond the lower entrance to the Clifton Rocks Railway, uniformed men stand on the steps of the Zig Zag in this view dating from around the time of the First World War. The Zig Zag, a steep winding path, was cut in St Vincent's Rocks to lead between the riverside at Hotwells and Clifton Down. In the background of this view is the station of the Port and Pier Railway, which was in operation between 1864 and 1922. The line ran from Hotwells to Avonmouth with stations at Sea Mills and Shirehampton.

162 This early photograph, showing the construction of Clifton Suspension Bridge, was taken from the top of the Clifton tower in 1863. It also shows the Avon Gorge with Leigh Woods on the opposite side. The bridge was opened on 8 December 1864, five years after the death of its designer, Isambard Kingdom Brunel.

163 The towers of Clifton Suspension Bridge are 86ft high, while the distance spanned by the chains is 702ft. The height of the carriageway above high tide is 245ft. It is estimated that the total cost of building the bridge was almost £100,000. This view of the bridge also shows the Somerset side of the Avon Gorge.

164 Bridge officials pose for the photographer in this early 20th-century view of the Clifton Suspension Bridge and its toll-booths. At this time, the tolls were: foot passengers, single journey 1d., return 2d.; bicycles 2d., return 3d.; carriages 6d., single or return. In 1909, it was envisaged that tolls to cross the bridge might come to an end in 1944, but they are still in force.

165 This view of the Avon Gorge, looking downstream, was taken from Clifton Suspension Bridge and dates from c.1913. The quarry on the right, known as the Great Quarry, was worked until 1877.

166 The Observatory, *c*.1909. An old windmill once stood on the site of the Observatory at Clifton Down. In the late 1820s, an artist called William West acquired the ruins of the mill from the Society of Merchant Venturers, at a nominal rent, and rebuilt the tower, equipping it with telescopes and a camera obscura. Visitors to the Observatory could see Dundry church tower towards the south-east, Bristol on the east, Redland to the north, King's Weston Park and Durdham Downs to the north-west and the Bristol Channel with the Welsh hills on the west.

167 This view of the River Avon from Shirehampton Park looks upstream towards the Avon Gorge and dates from *c*.1910. Shirehampton, on the banks of the Avon, was celebrated for the beautiful walks to be found in its vicinity.

168   The *George Inn* is prominent in this view of High Street, dating from *c.*1908, when Harry Hobb, advertising old beers, ales and stout, was victualler at the inn. The old inn was demolished and superseded by a new public house in 1929.

169   In 1911, Edward Albert Reed, watchmaker and jeweller, had premises in High Street. His shop sign is on the extreme left of this view. At this time, the striped barber's pole, next door, showed the establishment of Wilfred Bolwell, hairdresser. A sign above the premises and garments hanging outside indicated the shop of Charles Henry Budd, outfitter, while another sign advertised C.H. Hull, confectioner and baker. In the distance, the gabled Elizabethan House, with the ivy-covered chimney, was the residence of mason, John Flower. On the right-hand side of High Street, after the Elizabethan House, the first shop was that of Mrs Laura Mason, a general store. The second belonged to Frederick Beecroft, cash chemist. The next two establishments were branches of banks, the Union of London & Smith's Bank and the Capital & Counties Bank. The shops with awnings were those of Edwin George Siderfin, draper, and John R. Codrington, butcher. An agency of yet another bank, the Wilts & Dorset Banking Co., was the last in the row before the Wesleyan Methodist Chapel. On the right, the shop with the decorative lamps outside was that of Waite & Son, ironmongers.

PILL

170 In past times, a ferry linked the village of Pill with Shirehampton on the opposite bank of the river. Dating from c.1910, this view of Pill shows the steep ferry slipway, which was exposed when the tide ebbed. In 1911, John Henry Russell was the ferryman, while Thomas Joseph Russell kept the *Red Lion Inn*, the dormer-windowed building in the centre of the picture. To the right of the slipway is another of Pill's hostelries, *Waterloo House*, formerly known as *Waterloo Inn*. This was operated by Mrs Lucy Sambourne in 1911.

171 This early 20th-century view of pilot vessels in Pill Harbour looks across the river to the *Lamplighter's Hall* at Shirehampton. Grahame Farr, in *Somerset Harbours*, noted that almost all the pilot skiffs were built at Pill. Besides Rowles boatyard, there was also Cooper's boatyard at the head of the creek. In 1908, Bristol pilot skiffs were between 40ft and 50ft long and between 10ft and 14ft wide. Their draft was between 7ft and 10ft. These measurements were given by Captain George Buck, a retired pilot, in his reminiscences about life in a Bristol Channel pilot skiff, which were included in Peter J. Stuckey's *The Sailing Pilots of the Bristol Channel* (1999).

172   In *The Bristol Channel* (1955), Brian Waters wrote of the narrow alleys in Pill along which 'you meet old men in nautical caps for Pill above all the villages in England has been the parish of pilots'. At the time of the 1891 census, the inhabitants of the steep cobbled Lawford's Lane included Bristol pilot William Thomas, along with mariner James Thomas, general blacksmith Henry Newton, mariner James C. Buck and carrier James Parfitt.

173   Pill railway station was opened in 1867 and closed in 1964. The people in this Edwardian view are looking towards steam railmotor No. 58. Built in 1905, this was 70ft long and had a small steam engine at one end. Inside the carriage, there were two saloons. The entrance was in the centre of the carriage and there were retractable steps.

174 This early 20th-century view of Pill looks downriver towards Avonmouth. Today, the view has changed as now the Avonmouth Bridge, a twin steel box girder structure, carries the M5 motorway high over the river a little way downstream from Pill.

AVONMOUTH

175 Now known as Portview Road, the name of Port View was originally given to this road as the buildings in it looked over the first dock at Avonmouth. The twin-gabled building, with a sign hanging from the balcony, was the *Cambridge Temperance Hotel*. Next door was stationer, Thomas T. Howell. On the left, in the distance, can be seen the tower of Avonmouth Congregational Church, which was opened in 1902 and demolished in 1974.

176　This early 20th-century view shows Gloucester Road, leading to the entrance to Avonmouth Docks. The high steps in front of the shops were built as a barrier against floods. A sign for Avonmouth Post Office can be seen on the tall gabled 19th-century row of shops, while the premises in the foreground of the view include Cole and Pottow Ltd, Tailors, Victoria Dining Rooms, a hairdresser's shop displaying a sign 'Teeth Scientifically Extracted' and Stuckey's Bank.

177　A busy scene in Gloucester Road at the level crossing and footbridge of the Great Western Railway. In the background is the *Royal Hotel*. G.E. Barnard ran the hotel in 1901, while Alfred Brice was manager in 1911.

178 Avonmouth Dock, known initially as the Bristol Port and Channel Dock, was opened on 24 February 1877, having taken nine years to build from the cutting of the first sod. The engineer, J.B. Mackenzie, described the main features of the new dock:

> The lock is 454 feet in length, and 70 feet in width; the depth of water over the cills at high water of equinoctial spring tides is 42 feet; 37 feet 6 inches at ordinary spring tides; and 26 feet at ordinary neap tides … The dock is 1,400 feet in length and 500 feet in width, giving an available water area of 16 acres, and the depth of water to be maintained will not be less than 26 feet.

179 The Royal Edward Dock at Avonmouth was constructed between 1902 and 1908. It was opened by King Edward VII and Queen Alexandra on 9 July 1908. In a message on the back of this souvenir postcard, the sender wrote that if it was fine an evening drive would be taken to see the illuminations and decorations, adding, '£7,500 have been spent on the decorations <u>alone</u> I hear!' An account of the royal visit was also given. 'When the King & Queen stopped nearly opposite us, the children all stood up and sang two verses of "God Save the King" with a will, followed by round upon round of cheering and waving flags, handkerchiefs and programmes.' The schoolchildren of Bristol and their teachers were given chocolate boxes, supplied by J.S. Fry & Sons Ltd of Bristol, to commemorate the event.

180 This view shows the swing bridge over the junction cut, which linked both the old dock and the new one. Signs on the end of the bridge warned that vehicles had to keep to the centre of the bridge and that smoking was strictly prohibited.

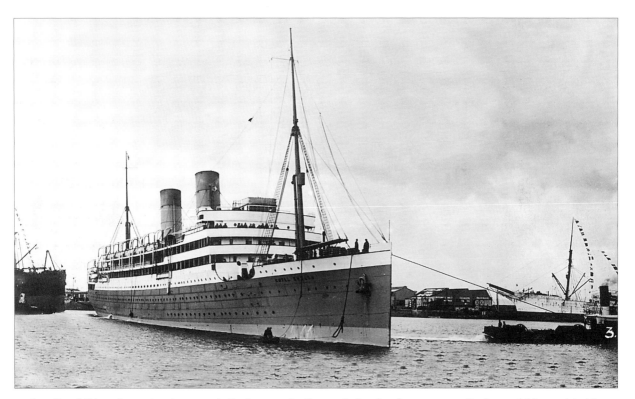

181 *Royal Edward*, entering Avonmouth Dock on 29 April 1910, before her first voyage to Quebec and Montreal in May 1910. Between 1910 and 1914, *Royal Edward* and her companion ship, *Royal George*, carried passengers to Canada every fortnight.

182 Royal Edward Dock, section of grain equipment, *c.*1920s. Among the cargoes landed at Avonmouth was grain from Canada. Large quantities of meat, butter and cheese were imported from far-flung places in the British Empire, while bananas were brought in from the West Indies, in huge consignments, by Elders and Fyffes.

Mouth of the Avon

183 The confluence of the River Avon with the River Severn surveyed from Penpole Point, a lofty height commanding an extensive view over the Severn and Welsh mountains. The viewpoint was such an attractive location for visitors in the 18th century that a Breakfasting Room was built there. This engraving was included in *A Brief Historical Sketch of Bristol with the New Picture of Clifton, and Stranger's Guide* by John Morgan. Besides the fine panorama, the Avon Lighthouse can be seen and the marshy ground, which eventually became used for the docks at the mouth of the River Avon.

Bibliography

Allsop, Niall, *Images of the Kennet & Avon 100 years in Camera Bristol to Bradford-on-Avon* (1987)

Allsop, Niall, *The Kennet & Avon Canal* (4th edn 1999)

Arrowsmith's Dictionary of Bristol (2nd edn. 1906)

Arrowsmith, J.W., *Guide to Bristol, Clifton & District* (1906)

Baddeley, M.J.B., *Bath and Bristol and Forty Miles Round* (1902)

Bailey's Western and Midland Directory (1783)

Barrett, William, *The History and Antiquities of the City of Bristol* (1789)

Bath and Bristol Guide, The (1755)

Bishop, Ian S., *Coal and the Dramway (within Rural Bitton)* (1999)

Bishop, Ian S., *Around Saltford* (2003)

Black, William, *The Strange Adventures of a House-Boat* (5th edn 1889)

Braine, A., *The History of Kingswood Forest* (1891)

Bristol and its Environs (1875)

Buchanan, R.A. and Cossons, Neil, *Industrial History in Pictures: Bristol* (1970)

Chilcott, J., *Chilcott's Descriptive History of Bristol* (1844)

Cliffe, Charles Frederick, *The Book of South Wales, The Bristol Channel, Monmouthshire, and The Wye* (1847)

Collinson, Rev. John, *The History and Antiquities of the County of Somerset* (1791)

De'Ath, Paul, *Images of England: Around Bradford-on-Avon* (2003)

Defoe, Daniel, *A Tour Thro' the Whole Island of Great Britain* (3rd edn 1742)

Farr, Grahame, *Bristol Shipbuilding in the Nineteenth Century* (1971)

Farr, Grahame, *Somerset Harbours* (1954)

Fassnidge, Harold, *Bradford on Avon Past and Present* (1993)

Freeman, Jane and Watkin, Aelred, *A History of Malmesbury* (1999)

Green, Colin, *Severn Traders* (1999)

Hill, John C. G., *Shipshape and Bristol Fashion* (1950s)

Hodge, Dr Bernulf, *A History of Malmesbury* (7th reprint 1998)

Hudson, John, *Towns and Villages of England: Tetbury* (1993)

Illustrated London News (1850, 1851)

Jones, Donald, *Bristol Past* (2000)

Jones, Roger, *Down the Bristol Avon* (1983)

Jones, W.H. and Jackson, J.E., annotated by Beddoe, John, *Bradford-on-Avon; A History and Description* (1907)

Latimer, John, *Annals of Bristol in the Eighteenth Century* (1893)

Latimer, John, *Annals of Bristol in the Nineteenth Century* (1887)

Lee, Rev. Alfred T., *The History of the Town and Parish of Tetbury* (1857)

Leech, Joseph, edited by Sutton, Alan, *Rural Rides of a Bristol Churchgoer* (1982)

Lewis, Brian, Fisher, Janet and Derek, *Bygone Bristol: Hotwells and the City Docks on old postcards* (nd)

Lord, John and Southam, Jem, *The Floating Harbour: A Landscape History of Bristol City Docks* (1983)

Lowe, Barbara and Brown, Tony, *Around Keynsham and Saltford in Old Photographs* (1988)

Matthews, William, *The New History Survey and Description of the City and Suburbs of Bristol or Complete Guide* (1794)

Morgan, John, *A Brief Historical Sketch of Bristol with the New Picture of Clifton, and Stranger's Guide* (1851)

National Trust, The, *Lacock* (1981, 2002)

Nicholls, J.F. and Taylor, John, *Bristol Past and Present* (1882 vol.3)

Nicholson Ordnance Survey Guide to the Waterways: Thames, Wey, Kennet & Avon (1997)

Pevsner, Nikolaus, *The Buildings of England: North Somerset and Bristol* (1958, 1973)

Platts, Arnold, *A History of Chippenham A.D. 853-1946* (nd)

Ports of the Bristol Channel, The (1893)

Reid, W. N. and Hicks, W.E., *Leading Events in the History of the Port of Bristol* (c.1877)

Rodgers, John, *English Rivers* (1947-8)

Rudder, Samuel, *New History of Gloucestershire* (1779)

Scott, Maurice, *Discovering Widcombe and Lyncombe, Bath* (1993)

Seyer, Samuel, *Memoirs Historical and Topographical of Bristol and its Neighbourhood* (1821 vol.1, 1823 vol.2)

Smith, Cyril Herbert, *Through the Kennet and Avon Canal by Motor Boat in 1928* (1929, 1990)

Stephenson, Dave, Jones, Andy, Willmott, Jill and Cheesley, Dave, *Images of England: Crews Hole, St George and Speedwell* (2003)

Stone, George Frederick, *Bristol: as it was and as it is* (1909)

Stone, Mike, *Images of England: Chippenham* (2003)

Stuckey, John, *A compleat history of Somersetshire* (1742)

Stuckey, Peter J., *The Sailing Pilots of the Bristol Channel* (1999)

Thomas, Ethel, *Down the 'Mouth: A History of Avonmouth* (1981)

Thomas, Ethel, *Shirehampton Story* (1983)

Tourist Guide to Bath (1927)

Twamley, Louisa Anne, *An Autumn Ramble by the Wye* (1839)
Walls, Ernest, *The Bristol Avon* (1927)
Ward, Lock & Co., *Guide to Bath, Cheddar, Wells, Glastonbury and District* (nd)
Waters, Brian, *The Bristol Channel* (1955)
Watson, Sally, *Secret Underground Bristol* (1991)
Wilson, Margaret, *The Limpley Stoke Valley* (1994)
Winstone, Reece, *Bath as it was* (1980)
Wood, John, *An Essay towards a Description of Bath* (1749)
Wright, Rev. G.N., *The Historic Guide to Bath* (1864)

Archive CD Books
J. Wright & Co.'s Bristol Directory (1901 CD 2001)
Kelly's Directory of Gloucestershire (1910 CD 2002)
Kelly's Directory of Somersetshire (1895 CD 2002)
Kelly's Directory of Somersetshire (1914 CD 2002)
Kelly's Directory of Wiltshire (1903 CD 2002)
Kelly's Directory of Wiltshire (1920 CD 2003)
Pigot & Co.'s Directory of Somerset & Bristol (1822 CD 2002)
Pigot & Co.'s Directory of Somerset (1842/1844, CD 2001)
The Universal British Directory of Trade, Commerce and Manufacture (1791, CD
    2001)

INDEX

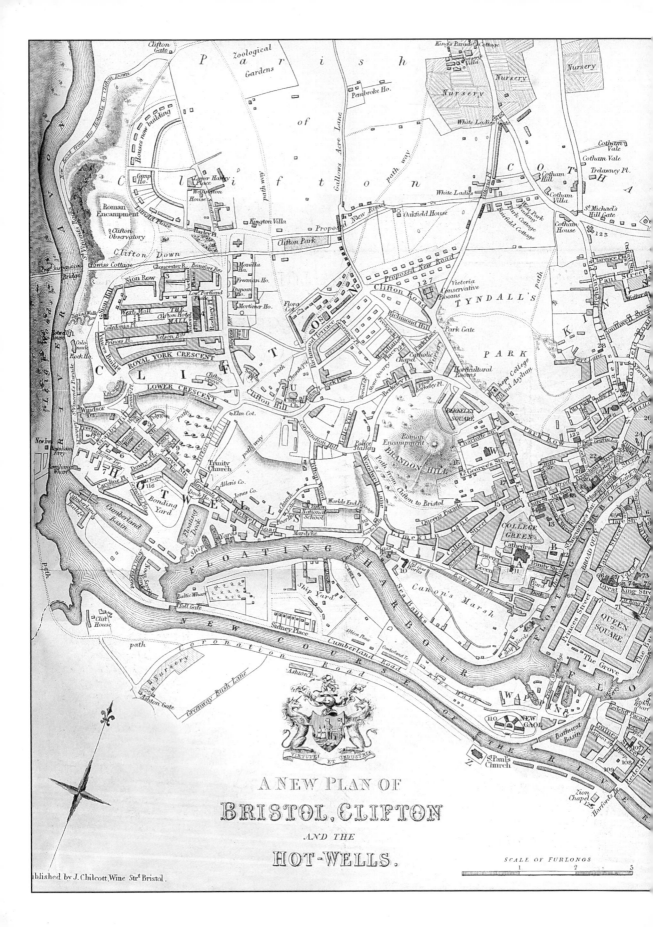

A NEW PLAN OF
BRISTOL, CLIFTON
AND THE
HOT-WELLS.

VIRTUTE ET INDUSTRIA

SCALE OF FURLONGS

Published by J. Chilcott, Wine Str.t Bristol.